Walter S. Landor, Ernest Radford

The Poems of Walter Savage Landor

Walter S. Landor, Ernest Radford

The Poems of Walter Savage Landor

ISBN/EAN: 9783337393687

Printed in Europe, USA, Canada, Australia, Japan

Cover: Foto ©Thomas Meinert / pixelio.de

More available books at **www.hansebooks.com**

THE POEMS OF WALTER SAVAGE LANDOR.

SELECTED AND EDITED BY ERNEST RADFORD.

LONDON :

WALTER SCOTT, 24 WARWICK LANE.

NEW YORK AND TORONTO :

W. I. GAGE & CO.

CONTENTS.

LANDOR.

THERE seems to be no need to prefix any words at all to my volume of Landor's verse. There is little to say that has not been said, and to the last word I do not aspire. The "last word" of criticism, my friend Mr. Birrell very shrewdly says, may be left to the "last man." It has been my wish to do something to bring the poetry of Landor within reach of the public, but here my desires have an end. I have not the showman's art. To preface a great author, to take the chair for a great speaker—to do these things to the admiration of practised editors, and incurable chairmen, requires an ampler prose than mine. If silence were really golden, as (sufficient) speech is silver, how gay were this paper life!

The hard task of an editor! He has not to celebrate his author—does Landor need praise of mine? He has to justify his own existence—to explain, as best he may, the obtrusion of his prose.

My volume is professedly of "Selections" from poems. I must make it clear that some principle has guided that selection.

I take from Mr. Colvin's book the words which Landor gives Boccaccio :—"What is there lovely in poetry unless there be moderation and composure? Are they not better than the hot, uncontrollable harlotry of a flaunting, dishevelled enthusiasm? Whoever has the power of creating, has likewise the inferior power of keeping his creations in order. The best poets are the most impressive because their steps are regular; for without regularity there is neither strength nor state. Look at Sophocles, look at Æschylus, look at Homer."

What Landor said so finely then cries out for a hearing now.

It is curious to note that Byron, the most reckless and least artistic of all the revolutionary school, was never quite happy in the freedom which his nature claimed, and which runs riot in his verse. We are all on the wrong tack, he exclaims. Ours is the Claudian, Pope's the Augustan age. He never tires of extolling *Rogers* as the surviving representative of what to him was the true school !

The badness of Byron's criticism is a common subject of talk amongst poetasters of to-day, who would also dethrone him as a poet. His little finger was thicker than their loins. Byron might as well have attempted to stop the course of Niagara as turn back the swollen flood of Poetry into its quiet accustomed channel. Nevertheless, his perception was sound, and true criticism lay hid beneath a petulant expression. The old school died of inanition, not because its methods were at fault.

To use a well-worn instance, the course of our literature, from the time of the Renaissance to that of the French Revolution, runs parallel with that of architecture in the same period. The exuberance of its first flood is checked. There succeeds the restrained and stately line of Milton. Dryden to Milton ; Pope to Dryden. So the architecture of Elizabeth, august yet vivacious withal, gives way to the Italian of Wren, more scholarly, but

with less of life. Next, we learn that to old Rome,
not modern Italy, we must go for a true standard
of style, and old Rome is re-edified again. So goes
this matter on; architecture and literature alike
failing beneath an "incubus of tradition," till in the
end when we think to have added the last graces
of style, lo, that which we would have adorned lies
dead! In place of a temple there stands a mauso-
leum. In place of living flowers to deck the warm
bosom of a bride a crackling artificial memorial
chaplet! Last, comes the Revolution, with the
effect of emancipating the world all at once from
a burden of old ideas, without all at once supply-
ing it with new. In scouting the subject-matter of
the old school, we scouted, and rightly, the forms
of it. The new wine was not for the old bottles,
but was it therefore to be spilt upon the plain?

Selections from *Gebir* guard the entrance to this
volume. There are fine passages. There are single
lines of majestic strength, in whose cadence is the
tramp of feet. But these beauties will not make
Gebir read to-day, and it was not by their strength
alone that a poem wholly unread by the many
secured almost in the hour of its appearance the
admiration and eager attention of the few.

It could not be said of Landor as Fuseli, in a large sort of broken English, was wont to say of Blake : " He is d—d good to steal from !" Southey found Landor, of all the poets of his own or of earlier days, the one who most completely defied imitation.

The poem was published, if publishing it could be called, in 1798, the year of the *Lyrical Ballads.* Landor in that year was twenty-three, Southey twenty-four, Coleridge twenty-six, Wordsworth twenty-eight. Byron, and Shelley, and Keats were children of ten years, and four, and three.

In connection with these dates the work must be considered. If any will contend that *Gebir* remains, in the largest sense, a great poem, I must leave it for him to say so. In face of the impossibility of reading it, I cannot say so much. What then is Landor's praise ?

His was that sheer Genius of Language which (for all their many words) our scholars so often lack. Landor appeared in a world of New Thought that was as yet but feebly articulate splendidly equipped for speech.

In mere fulness of life lies the need of sufficient expression. As enough is as good as a feast, so, in the case of an individual, "sufficient" may mean very little. But what, in a larger sense, is this "sufficient speech"? The question is the old question—What is style?

By virtue of his fuller life the poet is a Pioneer of Thought. In him the spirit of an age becomes vocal. _What it is his to proclaim, it is his to preserve._ (Oh, if Whitman, if Browning would think of this!) What speech shall suffice for him? Masterly presentation—in two words we find a criterion of style applicable to all arts alike. The artist, we may say, has a message. Style consists in its adequate—in its dignified delivery. The poet shapes his mother-tongue as the sculptor moulds our mother earth. Let his subject be what it may, his only concern as an artist is with its orderly fit presentment. This is his craft of speech. The _ars celare artem_ may be rendered thus—Style is not seen : it is felt.

The theme will change with changing Time ; but one law of art is eternal—the law which demands in the treatment of a subject what has been called a " Classical parsimony." The lightest touch of an artist, working in words or working in clay, must be deliberate in the afterthought.

"When I began to write *Gebir* I had just read Pindar a second time. What I admired was what nobody else had ever noticed—his proud complacency and scornful strength! If I could resemble him in nothing else, I was resolved to be as compendious and exclusive." It was this great language of his—compendious (up to the weight of any burden) and exclusive (not sticky with words) — that proclaimed him a master amongst masters of craft, and made him, as has been said, a poets' poet.

> ". . . O love !
> That thou couldst see my wars to-day, and knew'st
> The royal occupation, thou shouldst see
> A workman in't."

Thus speaks Antony to Cleopatra, as she arms him for the fight. The praise most precious to a writer comes from those who know something at least of his "royal occupation." Such men were the first (as they remain the sole) readers of *Gebir*. Such were Southey and Coleridge, De Quincey and Lamb. There were no more generous readers than these, and none so quick (as they "studied hard in their styles," like the students of Browning's poem), when Landor's verse was before them, to "see a workman in't."

Out of *Gebir* and into *Count Julian!* The drama was printed in 1812, and was received with delight by the same small group of great men as had hailed the appearance of the poem. Landor seems at that time to have indulged some hope that the play might be put upon the stage, and that Kemble might impersonate his hero. Thirty-four years later he had judged its dramatic qualities more exactly. In a note prefixed to *Count Julian*, in the "Collected Edition" of 1846, he says—"None of these poems of a dramatic form were offered to the stage, being no better than *Imaginary Conversations* in metre."

As far as this statement goes it must be considered final. And this evidently was Southey's view, who politely cloaked his opinion that an English audience would not stand it, by saying that it was so Greek.

Here is Landor's own account of its production: "In the day-time I laboured, and at night unburdened my mind, shedding many tears."

The work which was the result of an effort so noble as this will never be suffered to pass into the list of the "*biblia abiblia* — books which are no books;" nevertheless, as a whole, it may hardly be read. As it stands monumental, it remains unapproachable—a drama which is no drama.

Landor said repeatedly of his own poetry that it was, as compared with his prose, the work of an amateur. Literary critics too lightly, perhaps, have accepted this for a truth. I beg the best attention of my reader to this picture of Count Julian :—

> *Tarik.* At last
> He must be happy; for delicious calm
> Follows the fierce enjoyment of revenge.
>   *Hernando.* That calm was never his, no other will be.
> Thou knowest not, and mayst thou never know,
> How bitter is the tear that fiery shame
> Scourges and tortures from the soldier's eye.
> Whichever of these bad reports be true,
> He hides it from all hearts to wring his own,
> And drags the heavy secret to the grave.
> Not victory that o'ershadows him sees he ;
> No airy and light passion stirs abroad
> To ruffle or to soothe him ; all are quell'd
> Beneath a mightier, sterner stress of mind :
> Wakeful he sits, and lonely, and unmoved,
> Beyond the arrows, views, or shouts of men ;

LANDOR'S POEMS.

Gebir.

THE ARGUMENT OF GEBIR.

"THE intention of the poem is, by means of Gebir and his brother Tamar, to rebuke the ambition of conquest, however excusable its origin, and to reward the contests of peace, however at first unsuccessful.

Gebir is an Iberian Prince, Sovereign of Bœtic Spain, whose conquest of Egypt, undertaken to avenge the wrongs and assert the claims of his ancestors, is suspended through his love for its young Queen Charoba, by the treachery of whose nurse he is nevertheless slain amid the rejoicings of his marriage feast. Tamar is a shepherd youth, the keeper of his brother's herds and flocks, by whom nothing is so much cherished as to conquer to his love one of the Sea Nymphs, whom at first he vainly contends with, but who, made subject to mortal control by the superior power of his brother, yields to the passion already inspired in her, and carries Tamar to dwell with her for ever beyond the reach of human ambition."—FORSTER'S *Life of Landor.*

GEBIR.

FIRST BOOK.

I SING the fates of Gebir.   He had dwelt
Among those mountain-caverns which retain
His labours yet, vast halls and flowing wells,
Nor have forgotten their old master's name
Though sever'd from his people : here, incenst
By meditating on primeval wrongs,
He blew his battle-horn, at which uprose
Whole nations ; here, ten thousand of most might
He call'd aloud ; and soon Charoba saw
His dark helm hover o'er the land of Nile.
    What should the virgin do? should royal knees
Bend suppliant? or defenceless hands engage
Men of gigantic force, gigantic arms?
For 'twas reported that nor sword sufficed,
Nor shield immense nor coat of massive mail,
But that upon their towering heads they bore
Each a huge stone, refulgent as the stars.
This told she Dalica, then cried aloud,
" If on your bosom laying down my head

20 I sobb'd away the sorrows of a child,
  If I have always, and Heav'n knows I have,
  Next to a mother's held a nurse's name,
  Succour this one distress, recall those days,
  Love me, tho' 'twere because you lov'd me then."
   But whether confident in magic rites
  Or toucht with sexual pride to stand implor'd,
  Dalica smiled, then spake—"Away those fears.
  Though stronger than the strongest of his kind,
  He falls; on me devolve that charge; he falls.
30 Rather than fly him, stoop thou to allure;
  Nay, journey to his tents. A city stood
  Upon that coast, they say, by Sidad built,
  Whose father Gad built Gadir; on this ground
  Perhaps he sees an ample room for war.
  Persuade him to restore the walls himself
  In honour of his ancestors, persuade—
  But wherefore this advice? young, unespoused,
  Charoba want persuasions! and a queen!"
   "O Dalica!" the shuddering maid exclaim'd,
40 "Could I encounter that fierce frightful man?
  Could I speak? no, nor sigh." "And canst thou
   reign?"
  Cried Dalica; "yield empire or comply."
   Unfixt, though seeming fixt, her eyes downcast,
  The wonted buzz and bustle of the court
  From far through sculptured galleries met her ear,
  Then lifting up her head, the evening sun
  Pour'd a fresh splendour on her burnisht throne:
  The fair Charoba, the young queen, complied.

But Gebir, when he heard of her approach,
50　Laid by his orbed shield ; his vizor-helm,
His buckler and his corset he laid by,
And bade that none attend him : at his side
Two faithful dogs that urge the silent course,
Shaggy, deep-chested, croucht ; the crocodile,
Crying, oft made them raise their flaccid ears
And push their heads within their master's hand.
There was a brightening paleness in his face,
Such as Diana rising o'er the rocks
Shower'd on the lonely Latmian ; on his brow
60　Sorrow there was, yet nought was there severe.
But when the royal damsel first he saw,
Faint, hanging on her handmaid, and her knees
Tottering, as from the motion of the car,
His eyes lookt earnest on her, and those eyes
Show'd, if they had not, that they might have,
　　lov'd,
For there was pity in them at that hour.
With gentle speech, and more with gentle looks,
He sooth'd her ; but lest Pity go beyond
And crost Ambition lose her lofty aim,
70　Bending, he kist her garment, and retired.
He went, nor slumber'd in the sultry noon,
When viands, couches, generous wines, persuade,
And slumber most refreshes ; nor at night,
When heavy dews are laden with disease ;
And blindness waits not there for lingering age.
Ere morning dawn'd behind him, he arrived
At those rich meadows where young Tamar fed

The royal flocks entrusted to his care.
"Now," said he to himself, "will I repose
80 At least this burthen on a brother's breast."
His brother stood before him : he, amazed,
Rear'd suddenly his head, and thus began.
"Is it thou, brother!   Tamar, is it thou!
Why, standing on the valley's utmost verge,
Lookest thou on that dull and dreary shore
Where beyond sight Nile blackens all the sand?
And why that sadness?   When I past our sheep
The dew-drops were not shaken off the bar,
Therefore if one be wanting, 'tis untold."
90   "Yes, one is wanting, nor is that untold,"
Said Tamar; "and this dull and dreary shore
Is neither dull nor dreary at all hours."
Whereon the tear stole silent down his cheek,
Silent, but not by Gebir unobserv'd :
Wondering he gazed awhile, and pitying spake.
"Let me approach thee ; does the morning light
Scatter this wan suffusion o'er thy brow,
This faint blue lustre under both thine eyes?"
    "O brother, is this pity or reproach?"
100 Cried Tamar, "cruel if it be reproach,
If pity, O how vain!"   "Whate'er it be
That grieves thee, I will pity, thou but speak,
And I can tell thee, Tamar, pang for pang."
    "Gebir! then more than brothers are we now!
Everything (take my hand) will I confess.
I neither feed the flock nor watch the fold ;
How can I, lost in love?   But, Gebir, why

That anger which has risen to your cheek?
Can other men? could you? what, no reply!
110 And still more anger, and still worse conceal'd!
Are these your promises? your pity this?"
    "Tamar, I well·may pity what I feel—
Mark me aright—I feel for thee—proceed—
Relate me all." "Then will I all relate,"
Said the young shepherd, gladden'd from his heart.
    "'Twas evening, though not sunset, and the tide
Level with these green meadows, seem'd yet higher:
'Twas pleasant; and I loosen'd from my neck
The pipe you gave me, and began to play.
120 O that I ne'er had learnt the tuneful art!
It always brings us enemies or love.
Well, I was playing, when above the waves
Some swimmer's head methought I saw ascend;
I, sitting still, survey'd it, with my pipe
Awkwardly held before my lips half-closed,
Gebir! it was a Nymph! a Nymph divine!
I cannot wait describing how she came,
How I was sitting, how she first assum'd
The sailor; of what happen'd there remains
130 Enough to say, and too much to forget.
The sweet deceiver stept upon this bank
Before I was aware; for with surprise
Moments fly rapid as with love itself.
Stooping to tune afresh the hoarsen'd reed,
I heard a rustling, and where that arose
My glance first lighted on her nimble feet.
Her feet resembled those long shells explored

By him who to befriend his steed's dim sight
Would blow the pungent powder in the eye.
140 Her eyes too ! O immortal Gods ! her eyes
Resembled—what could they resemble ? what
Ever resemble those ?   Even her attire
Was not of wonted woof nor vulgar art :
Her mantle show'd the yellow samphire-pod,
Her girdle the dove-colour'd wave serene.
' Shepherd,' said she, ' and will you wrestle now,
And with the sailor's hardier race engage ?'
I was rejoiced to hear it, and contrived
How to keep up contention : could I fail
150 By pressing not too strongly, yet to press ?
' Whether a shepherd, as indeed you seem,
Or whether of the hardier race you boast,
I am not daunted ; no ; I will engage.'
' But first,' said she, ' what wager will you lay ?'
' A sheep,' I answered : ' add whate'er you will.'
' I cannot,' she replied, ' make that return :
Our hided vessels in their pitchy round
Seldom, unless from rapine, hold a sheep.
But I have sinuous shells of pearly hue
160 Within, and they that lustre have imbibed
In the sun's palace-porch, where when unyoked
His chariot-wheel stands midway in the wave :
Shake one and it awakens, then apply
Its polisht lips to your attentive ear,
And it remembers its august abodes,
And murmurs as the ocean murmurs there.
And I have others given me by the nymphs,

Of sweeter sound than any pipe you have;
But we, by Neptune! for no pipe contend,
170 This time a sheep I win, a pipe the next.'
Now came she forward eager to engage,
But first her dress, her bosom then survey'd,
And heav'd it, doubting if she could deceive.
Her bosom seem'd, inclos'd in haze like heav'n,
To baffle touch, and rose forth undefined;
Above her knee she drew the robe succinct,
Above her breast, and just below her arms.
'This will preserve my breath when tightly bound,
If struggle and equal strength should so con-
 strain.'
180 Thus, pulling hard to fasten it, she spake,
And, rushing at me, closed: I thrill'd throughout
And seem'd to lessen and shrink up with cold.
Again with violent impulse gusht my blood,
And hearing nought external, thus absorb'd,
I heard it, rushing through each turbid vein,
Shake my unsteady swimming sight in air.
Yet with unyielding though uncertain arms
I clung around her neck; the vest beneath
Rustled against our slippery limbs entwined:
190 Often mine springing with eluded force
Started aside and trembled till replaced:
And when I most succeeded, as I thought,
My bosom and my throat felt so comprest
That life was almost quivering on my lips,
Yet nothing was there painful: these are signs
Of secret arts and not of human might;

What arts I cannot tell; I only know
My eyes grew dizzy and my strength decay'd;
I was indeed o'ercome . . with what regret,
200 And more, with what confusion, when I reacht
The fold, and yielding up the sheep, she cried,
' This pays a shepherd to a conquering maid.'
She smiled, and more of pleasure than disdain
Was in her dimpled chin and liberal lip,
And eyes that languisht, lengthening, just like love.
She went away; I on the wicker gate
Leant, and could follow with my eyes alone.
The sheep she carried easy as a cloak;
But when I heard its bleating, as I did,
210 And saw, she hastening on, its hinder feet
Struggle, and from her snowy shoulder slip,
One shoulder its poor efforts had unveil'd,
Then all my passions mingling fell in tears;
Restless then ran I to the highest ground
To watch her; she was gone; gone down the tide;
And the long moon-beam on the hard wet sand
Lay like a jasper column half up-rear'd."
  " But, Tamar! tell me, will she not return?'
  " She will return, yet not before the moon
220 Again is at the full: she promist this,
Tho' when she promist I could not reply."
  " By all the Gods I pity thee! go on,
Fear not my anger, look not on my shame,
For when a lover only hears of love
He finds his folly out, and is ashamed.
Away with watchful nights and lonely days,

Contempt of earth and aspect up to heaven,
With contemplation, with humility,
A tatter'd cloak that pride wears when deform'd,
230 Away with all that hides me from myself,
Parts me from others, whispers I am wise:
From our own wisdom less is to be reapt
Than from the barest folly of our friend.
Tamar! thy pastures, large and rich, afford
Flowers to thy bees and herbage to thy sheep,
But, battened on too much, the poorest croft
Of thy poor neighbour yields what thine denies."
   They hasten'd to the camp, and Gebir there
Resolved his native country to forego,
240 And order'd from those ruins to the right
They forthwith raise a city.   Tamar heard
With wonder, tho' in passing 'twas half-told,
His brother's love, and sigh'd upon his own.

———

SECOND BOOK.

Gebir overcomes the Sea Nymph beloved of Tamar.

   .   .   .   .   . THEY parted here:
And Gebir, bending through the woodland, cull'd
The creeping vine and viscous raspberry,
Less green and less compliant than they were,
And twisted in those mossy tufts that grow
On brakes of roses when the roses fade:
And as he passes on, the little hinds

That shake for bristly herds the foodful bough,
110 Wonder, stand still, gaze, and trip satisfied ;
Pleas'd more if chestnut, out of prickly husk
Shot from the sandal, roll along the glade.
  And thus unnoticed went he, and untired
Stept up the acclivity; and as he stept,
And as the garlands nodded o'er his brow,
Sudden from under a close alder sprang
Th' expectant nymph, and seiz'd him unaware.
He stagger'd at the shock ; his feet at first
Slipt backward from the wither'd grass shortgrazed,
120 But striking out one arm, tho' without aim,
Then grasping with his other, he enclosed
The struggler ; she gain'd not one step's retreat,
Urging with open hands against his throat
Intense, now holding in her breath constrain'd,
Now pushing with quick impulse and by starts,
Till the dust blacken'd upon every pore.
Nearer he drew her and yet nearer, claspt
Above the knees midway, and now one arm
Fell, and her other lapsing o'er the neck
130 Of Gebir, swung against his back incurved,
The swoln veins glowing deep, and with a groan
On his broad shoulder fell her face reclined.
But ah ! she knew not whom that roseate face
Cool'd with its breath ambrosial ; for she stood
Higher on the bank, and often swept and broke
His chaplets mingled with her loosen'd hair.
  Whether, while Tamar tarried, came desire,
As she, grown languid, loost the wings of Love

Which she before held proudly at her will,
140 And, nought but Tamar in her soul, and nought
(Where Tamar was) that seem'd or fear'd deceit,
To fraud she yielded what no force had gain'd ;
Or whether Jove in pity to mankind,
When from his crystal fount the visual orbs
He fill'd with piercing ether, and endued
With somewhat of omnipotence, ordain'd
That never two fair forms at once torment
The human heart and draw it different ways,
And thus, in prowess like a god, the chief
150 Subdued her strength nor softened at her charms,
The nymph divine, the magic mistress, fail'd.
Recovering, still half-resting on the turf,
She lookt up wildly, and could now descry
The kingly brow archt lofty for command.

.   .   .   .   .   .

SEVENTH BOOK.

The Death of Gebir.

.   .   .   .   .   .

THE long-awaited day at last arrived
When, linkt together by the seven-armed Nile,
Egypt with proud Iberia should unite.
Here the Tartessian, there the Gadite tents
Rang with impatient pleasure : here engaged
Woody Nebrissa's quiver-bearing crew,
Contending warm with amicable skill,

While they of Durius raced along the beach
And scatter'd mud and jeers on all behind.
50   The strength of Bætis too removed the helm
And stript the corselet off, and stauncht the foot
Against the mossy maple, while they tore
Their quivering lances from the hissing wound.
Others push forth the prows of their compeers,
And the wave, parted by the pouncing beak,
Swells up the sides and closes far astern :
The silent oars now dip their level wings,
And weary with strong stroke the whitening wave.
Others, afraid of tardiness, return :
60   Now, entering the still harbour, every surge
Runs with a louder murmur up their keel,
And the slack cordage rattles round the mast.
Sleepless with pleasure and expiring fears
Had Gebir risen ere the break of dawn,
And o'er the plains appointed for the feast
Hurried with ardent step : the swains admired
What so transversely could have swept the dew ;
For never long one path had Gebir trod,
Nor long, unheeding man, one pace preserv'd.
70   Not thus Charoba : she despair'd the day ;
The day was present ; true ; yet she despair'd.
In the too tender and once tortured heart
Doubts gather strength from habit, like disease ;
Fears, like the needle verging to the pole,
Tremble and tremble into certainty.
How often, when her maids with merry voice
Call'd her, and told the sleepless queen 'twas morn,

How often would she feign some fresh delay,
And tell 'em (though they saw) that she arose.
80 Next to her chamber, closed by cedar doors,
A bath of purest marble, purest wave,
On its fair surface bore its pavement high :
Arabian gold enchased the crystal roof,
With fluttering boys adorn'd and girls unrobed ;
These, when you touch the quiet water, start
From their aërial sunny arch, and pant
Entangled mid each other's flowery wreaths,
And each pursuing is in turn pursued.
Here came at last, as ever wont at morn,
90 Charoba : long she lingered at the brink,
Often she sigh'd, and, naked as she was,
Sate down, and leaning on the couch's edge,
On the soft inward pillow of her arm
Rested her burning cheek : she moved her eyes;
She blusht ; and blushing plunged into the wave.
Now brazen chariots thunder through each street,
And neighing steeds paw proudly from delay.
While o'er the palace breathes the dulcimer,
Lute, and aspiring harp, and lisping reed,
100 Loud rush the trumpets bursting through the throng
And urge the high-shoulder'd vulgar; now are heard
Curses and quarrels and constricted blows,
Threats and defiance and suburban war.
Hark ! the reiterated clangour sounds !
Now murmurs, like the sea or like the storm
Or like the flames on forests, move and mount
From rank to rank, and loud and louder roll,

Till all the people is one vast applause.
Yes, 'tis herself, Charoba.   Now the strife
110 To see again a form so often seen.
Feel they some partial pang, some secret void,
Some doubt of feasting those fond eyes again?
Panting imbibe they that refreshing sight
To reproduce in hour of bitterness?
She goes, the king awaits her from the camp :
Him she descried, and trembled ere he reacht
Her car, but shuddered paler at his voice.
So the pale silver at the festive board
Grows paler fill'd afresh and dew'd with wine ;
120 So seems the tenderest herbage of the spring
To whiten, bending from a balmy gale.
The beauteous queen alighting he received,
And sigh'd to loose her from his arms ; she hung
A little longer on them through her fears.
Her maidens follow'd her ; and one that watcht,
One that had call'd her in the morn, observ'd
How virgin passion with unfuel'd flame
Burns into whiteness, while the blushing cheek
Imagination heats and shame imbues.
130   Between both nations drawn in ranks they pass :
The priests, with linen ephods, linen robes,
Attend their steps, some follow, some precede,
Where clothed with purple intertwined with gold
Two lofty thrones commanded land and main.
Behind and near them numerous were the tents
As freckled clouds o'erfloat our vernal skies,
Numerous as wander in warm moonlight nights

Along Meänder's or Caÿster's marsh
Swans pliant-neckt and village storks revered.
140 Throughout each nation moved the hum confused,
Like that from myriad wings o'er Scythian cups
Of frothy milk, concreted soon with blood.
Throughout the fields the savoury smoke ascends,
And boughs and branches shade the hides unbroacht.
Some roll the flowery turf into a seat,
And others press the helmet.   Now resounds
The signal ! queen and monarch mount the thrones.
The brazen clarion hoarsens : many leagues
Above them, many to the south, the heron
150 Rising with hurried croak and throat outstretcht,
Ploughs up the silvering surface of her plain.
    Tottering with age's zeal and mischief's haste
Now was discover'd Dalica ; she reacht
The throne, she leant against the pedestal,
And now ascending stood before the king.
Prayers for his health and safety she preferr'd,
And o'er his head and o'er his feet she threw
Myrrh, nard, and cassia, from three golden urns ;
His robe of native woof she next removed,
160 And round his shoulders drew the garb accurst,
And bow'd her head, departing : soon the queen
Saw the blood mantle in his manly cheeks,
And fear'd, and faltering sought her lost replies,
And blest the silence that she wisht were broke.
Alas, unconscious maiden ! night shall close,
And love and sovranty and life dissolve,
And Egypt be one desert drencht in blood.

When thunder overhangs the fountain-head,
Losing its wonted freshness every stream
170 Grows turbid, grows with sickly warmth suffused :
Thus were the brave Iberians when they saw
The king of nations from his throne descend.
Scarcely, with pace uneven, knees unnerv'd,
Reacht he the waters : in his troubled ear
They sounded murmuring drearily ; they rose
Wild, in strange colours, to his parching eyes ;
They seem'd to rush around him, seem'd to lift
From the receding earth his helpless feet.
He fell : Charoba shriekt aloud ; she ran ;
180 Frantic with fears and fondness, mazed with woe,
Nothing but Gebir dying she beheld.
The turban that betray'd its golden charge
Within, the veil that down her shoulder hung,
All fallen at her feet ! the furthest wave
Creeping with silent progress up the sand,
Glided through all, and rais'd their hollow folds.
In vain they bore him to the sea, in vain
Rubb'd they his temples with the briny warmth ;
He struggled from them, strong with agony,
190 He rose half up, he fell again, he cried
" *Charoba! O Charoba!* " She embraced
His neck, and raising on her knee one arm,
Sigh'd when it moved not, when it fell she shriek:,
And clasping loud both hands above her head,
She call'd on Gebir, call'd on earth, on heaven.
    " Who will believe me ? what shall I protest ?
How innocent, thus wretched ? God of Gods,

Strike me—who most offend thee most defy—
Charoba most offends thee : strike me, hurl
200 From this accursed land this faithless throne.
O Dalica ! see here the royal feast !
See here the gorgeous robe ! you little thought
How have the demons dyed that robe with death.
Where are ye, dear fond parents ! when ye heard
My feet in childhood pat the palace-floor,
Ye started forth and kist away surprise :
Will ye now meet me ? how, and where, and when ?
And must I fill your bosom with my tears,
And, what I never have done, with your own?
210 Why have the Gods thus punisht me ? what harm
Have ever I done them ? have I profaned
Their temples, askt too little, or too much?
Proud if they granted, griev'd if they withheld ?
O mother ! stand between your child and them !
Appease them, soothe them, soften their revenge,
Melt them to pity with maternal tears.
Alas, but if you cannot ! they themselves
Will then want pity rather than your child.
O Gebir ! best of monarchs, best of men,
220 What realm hath ever thy firm even hand
Or lost by feebleness or held by force ?
Behold thy cares and perils how repaid !
Behold the festive day, the nuptial hour ! '
    Thus raved Charoba : horror, grief, amaze,
Pervaded all the host ; all eyes were fixt ;
All stricken motionless and mute : the feast
Was like the feast of Cepheus, when the sword

Of Phineus, white with wonder, shook restrain'd,
And the hilt rattled in his marble hand.
230 She heard not, saw not, every sense was gone;
One passion banisht all; dominion, praise,
The world itself, was nothing.   Senseless man !
What would thy fancy figure now from worlds?
There is no world to those that grieve and love.
She hung upon his bosom, prest his lips,
Breath'd, and would feign it his that she resorb'd,
She chafed the feathery softness of his veins,
That swell'd out black, like tendrils round their
    vase
After libation : lo ! he moves ! he groans !
240 He seems to struggle from the grasp of death !
Charoba shriekt and fell away, her hand
Still clasping his, a sudden blush o'erspread
Her pallid humid cheek, and disappear'd.
'Twas not the blush of shame; what shame has
    woe ?
'Twas not the genuine ray of hope; it flasht
With shuddering glimmer through unscatter'd
    clouds,
It flasht from passions rapidly opposed.
    Never so eager, when the world was waves,
Stood the less daughter of the ark, and tried
250 (Innocent this temptation !) to recall
With folded vest and casting arm the dove ;
Never so fearful, when amid the vines
Rattled the hail, and when the light of heaven
Closed, since the wreck of Nature, first eclipst,

As she was eager for his life's return,
As she was fearful how his groans might end.
They ended : cold and languid calm succeeds ;
His eyes have lost their lustre, but his voice
Is not unheard, though short : he spake these
    words.
260   " And weepest thou, Charoba ! shedding tears
More precious than the jewels that surround
The neck of kings entomb'd ! then weep, fair queen,
At once thy pity and my pangs assuage.
Ah ! what is grandeur ? glory ? they are past !
When nothing else, not life itself, remains,
Still the fond mourner may be call'd our own.
Should I complain of Fortune ? how she errs,
Scattering her bounty upon barren ground,
Slow to allay the lingering thirst of toil ?
270 Fortune, 'tis true, may err, may hesitate,
Death follows close nor hesitates nor errs.
I feel the stroke ! I die ! " He would extend
His dying arm : it fell upon his breast ;
Cold sweat and shivering ran o'er every limb,
His eyes grew stiff, he struggled, and expired.

Count Julian.

CHARACTERS.

COUNT JULIAN. RODERIGO, *King of Spain.* OPAS, *Metropolitan of Seville.* SISABERT, *betrothed to* COVILLA. MUZA, *Prince of Mauritania.* ABDALAZIS, *son of* MUZA. TARIK, *Moorish Chieftain.* COVILLA,* *daughter of* JULIAN. EGILONA, *wife of* RODERIGO. HERNANDO, OSMA, RAMIRO, *etc., Officers.*

---

* The daughter of Count Julian is usually called Florinda. The city of Covilla, it is reported, was named after her. Here is no improbability: there would be a gross one in deriving the word, as is also pretended, from La Cava. Cities, in adopting a name, bear it usually as a testimony of victories or as an augury of virtues. Small and obscure places occasionally receive what their neighbours throw against them; as *Puerto de la mala muger* in Mercia: but a generous people would affix no stigma to innocence and misfortune. It is remarkable that the most important era in Spanish history should be the most obscure. This is propitious to the poet, and above all to the tragedian. Few characters of such an era can be glaringly misrepresented, few facts offensively perverted.

COUNT JULIAN.

——◆——

FIRST ACT : FIRST SCENE.

Camp of Julian.

OPAS. JULIAN.

Opas. See her, Count Julian : if thou lovest God,
See thy lost child.
   Julian.   I have avenged me, Opas,
More than enough : l only sought to hurl
The brands of war on one detested head,
And die upon his ruin.   O my country !
O lost to honour, to thyself, to me,
Why on barbarian hands devolves thy cause,
Spoilers, blasphemers !
    Opas.   Is it thus, Don Julian,
When thy own offspring, that beloved child
For whom alone these very acts were done
By them and thee, when thy Covilla stands
An outcast and a suppliant at thy gate,
Why that still stubborn agony of soul,
Those struggles with the bars thyself imposed ?
Is she not thine ? not dear to thee as ever ?

Julian. Father of mercies ! show me none, whene'er
The wrongs she suffers cease to wring my heart,
Or I seek solace ever, but in death.
    Opas. What wilt thou do then, too unhappy man?
    Julian. What have I done already?   All my peace
Has vanisht ; my fair fame in aftertime
Will wear an alien and uncomely form,
Seen o'er the cities I have laid in dust,
Countrymen slaughtered, friends abjured !
    Opas.   And faith?
    Julian. Alone now left me, filling up in part
The narrow and waste intervals of grief :
It promises that I shall see again
My own lost child.
    Opas.   Yes, at this very hour.
    Julian. Till I have met the tyrant face to face,
And gain'd a conquest greater than the last ;
Till he no longer rules one rood of Spain,
And not one Spaniard, not one enemy,
The least relenting, flags upon his flight ;
Till we are equal in the eyes of men,
The humblest and most wretched of our kind,
No peace for me, no comfort, no—no child !
    Opas. No pity for the thousands fatherless,
The thousands childless like thyself, nay more,
The thousands friendless, helpless, comfortless—
Such thou wilt make them, little thinking so,
Who now perhaps, round their first winter fire,
Banish, to talk of thee, the tales of old,
Shedding true honest tears for thee unknown :

Precious be these and sacred in thy sight,
Mingle them not with blood from hearts thus kind.
If only warlike spirits were evoked
By the war-demon, I would not complain,
Or dissolute and discontented men ;
But wherefore hurry down into the square
The neighbourly, saluting, warm-clad race,
Who would not injure us, and cannot serve ;
Who, from their short and measured slumber risen,
In the faint sunshine of their balconies,
With a half-legend of a martyrdom
And some weak wine and withered grapes before
        them,
Note by their foot the wheel of melody
That catches and rolls on the Sabbath dance.
To drag the steady prop from failing age,
Break the young stem that fondness twines around,
Widen the solitude of lonely sighs,
And scatter to the broad bleak wastes of day
The ruins and the phantoms that replied,
Ne'er be it thine.
  Julian.   Arise, and save me, Spain !

FIRST ACT: SECOND SCENE.

*   Muza *enters.*

Muza. Infidel chief, thou tarriest here too long,
And art perhaps repining at the days
Of nine continued victories o'er men

Dear to thy soul, tho' reprobate and base.
Away !   [*He retires.*

Julian. I follow. Could my bitterest foes
Hear this ! ye Spaniards, this ! which I foreknew
And yet encounter'd ; could they see your Julian
Receiving orders from and answering
These desperate and heaven-abandoned slaves,
They might perceive some few external pangs,
Some glimpses of the hell wherein I move,
Who never have been fathers.

Opas.   These are they
To whom brave Spaniards must refer their wrongs !

Julian. Muza, that cruel and suspicious chief,
Distrusts his friends more than his enemies,
Me more than either ; fraud he loves and fears,
And watches her still footfall day and night.

Opas. O Julian ! such a refuge ! such a race !

Julian. ——Calamities like mine alone implore.
No virtues have redeem'd them from their bonds ;
Wily ferocity, keen idleness,
And the close cringes of ill-whispering want,
Educate them to plunder and obey :
Active to serve him best whom most they fear,
They show no mercy to the merciful,
And racks alone remind them of the name.

Opas. O everlasting curse for Spain and thee !

Julian. Spain should have vindicated then her
          wrongs
In mine, a Spaniard's and a soldier's wrongs.

Opas. Julian, are thine the only wrongs on earth ?

And shall each Spaniard rather vindicate
Thine than his own ? is there no Judge of all ?
Shall mortal hand seize with impunity
The sword of vengeance from the armoury
Of the Most High ? easy to wield, and starred
With glory it appears ; but all the host
Of the archangels, should they strive at once,
Would never close again its widening blade.

Julian. He who provokes it hath so much to rue.
Where'er he turn, whether to earth or heaven,
He finds an enemy, or raises one.

Opas. I never yet have seen where long success
Hath followed him who warred upon his king.

Julian. Because the virtue that inflicts the stroke
Dies with him, and the rank ignoble heads
Of plundering faction soon unite again,
And prince-protected share the spoil at rest.

FIRST ACT: THIRD SCENE.

Guard announces a Herald. OPAS *departs.*

Guard. A messenger of peace is at the gate,
My lord, safe access, private audience,
And free return, he claims.
Julian.   Conduct him in.

RODERIGO *enters as a herald.*

A messenger of peace ! audacious man !

In what attire appearest thou ? a herald's ?
Under no garb can such a wretch be safe.
  Roderigo. Thy violence and fancied wrongs I know,
And what thy sacrilegious hands would do,
O traitor and apostate !
  Julian.   What they would
They cannot : thee of kingdom and of life
'Tis easy to despoil, thyself the traitor,
Thyself the violator of allegiance.
O would all-righteous Heaven they could restore
The joy of innocence, the calm of age,
The probity of manhood, pride of arms,
And confidence of honour ! the august
And holy laws trampled beneath thy feet,
And Spain ! O parent, I have lost thee too !
Yes, thou wilt curse me in thy latter days,
Me, thine avenger.   I have fought her foe,
Roderigo, I have gloried in her sons,
Sublime in hardihood and piety :
Her strength was mine : I, sailing by her cliffs,
By promontory after promontory,
Opening like flags along some castle-tower,
Have sworn before the cross upon our mast
Ne'er shall invader wave his standard there.
  Roderigo. Yet there thou plantest it, false man,
        thyself.
  Julian. Accursed he who makes me this reproach,
And made it just !   Had I been happy still,
I had been blameless : I had died with glory
Upon the walls of Ceuta.

Roderigo.   Which thy treason
Surrendered to the Infidel.
   Julian.   'Tis hard
And base to live beneath a conqueror;
Yet, amid all this grief and infamy,
'Twere something to have rusht upon the ranks
In their advance; 'twere something to have stood
Defeat, discomfiture, and, when around
No beacon blazes, no far axle groans
Thro' the wide plain, no sound of sustenance
Or succour soothes the still-believing ear,
To fight upon the last dismantled tower,
And yield to valour, if we yield at all.
But rather should my neck lie trampled down
By every Saracen and Moor on earth,
Than my own country see her laws o'erturn'd
By those who should protect them.   Sir, no prince
Shall ruin Spain, and, least of all, her own.
Is any just or glorious act in view,
Your oaths forbid it: is your avarice,
Or, if there be such, any viler passion
To have its giddy range and to be gorged,
It rises over all your sacraments,
A hooded mystery, holier than they all.
   Roderigo. Hear me, Don Julian; I have heard thy
      wrath
Who am thy king, nor heard man's wrath before.
   Julian. Thou shalt hear mine, for thou art not my
      king.
   Roderigo. Knowest thou not the altered face of war?

Xeres is ours ; from every region round
True loyal Spaniards throng into our camp :
Nay, thy own friends and thy own family,
From the remotest provinces, advance
To crush rebellion : Sisabert is come;
Disclaiming thee and thine ; the Asturian hills
Oppose to him their icy chains in vain:
But never wilt thou see him, never more,
Unless in adverse war and deadly hate.

   Julian. So lost to me ! so generous, so deceived !
I grieve to hear it.

   Roderigo.   Come, I offer grace,
Honour, dominion: send away these slaves,
Or leave them to our sword, and all beyond
The distant Ebro to the towns of France
Shall bless thy name and bend before thy throne.
I will myself accompany thee, I,
The king, will hail thee brother.

   Julian.   Ne'er shalt thou
Henceforth be king: the nation in thy name
May issue edicts, champions may command
The vassal multitudes of marshal'd war,
And the fierce charger shrink before the shouts,
Lower'd as if earth had open'd at his feet,
While thy mail'd semblance rises tow'rd the ranks,
But God alone sees thee.

   Roderigo.   What hopest thou ?
To conquer Spain, and rule a ravaged land?
To compass me around? to murder me ?   [fight

   Julian. No, Don Roderigo : swear thou, in the

That thou wilt meet me, hand to hand, alone,
That, if I ever save thee from a foe——
   Roderigo. I swear what honour asks. First, to Covilla
Do thou present my crown and dignity.
   Julian. Darest thou offer any price for shame?
   Roderigo. Love and repentance.
   Julian.   Egilona lives;
And were she buried with her ancestors,
Covilla should not be the gaze of men,
Should not, despoil'd of honour, rule the free.
   Roderigo. Stern man! her virtues well deserve the
      throne.
   Julian. And Egilona, what hath she deserv'd,
The good, the lovely?
   Roderigo.   But the realm in vain
Hoped a succession.
   Julian.   Thou hast torn away
The root of royalty.
   Roderigo.   For her, for thee.
   Julian. Blind insolence! base insincerity!
Power and renown no mortal ever shared
Who could retain or grasp them to himself:
And, for Covilla? patience! peace! for her?
She call upon her God, and outrage him
At his own altar! *she* repeat the vows
She violates in repeating! who abhors
Thee and thy crimes, and wants no crown of thine.
Force may compel the abhorrent soul, or want
Lash and pursue it to the public ways;
Virtue looks back and weeps, and may return

To these, but never near the abandon'd one
Who drags religion to adultery's feet,
And rears the altar higher for her sake.
 Roderigo. Have then the Saracens possest thee
  quite ?
And wilt thou never yield me thy consent ?
 Julian. Never.
 Roderigo.   So deep in guilt, in treachery !
Forced to acknowledge it ! forced to avow
The traitor !
 Julian.   Not to thee, who reignest not,
But to a country ever dear to me,
And dearer now than ever ! What we love
Is loveliest in departure ! One I thought,
As every father thinks, the best of all,
Graceful and mild and sensible and chaste :
Now all these qualities of form and soul
Fade from before me, nor on any one
Can I repose, or be consoled by any.
And yet in this torn heart I love her more
Than I could love her when I dwelt on each,
Or claspt them all united, and thankt God,
Without a wish beyond. Away, thou fiend !
O ignominy, last and worst of all !
I weep before thee—like a child—like mine—
And tell my woes, fount of them all ! to thee !

———

FIRST ACT : FOURTH SCENE.

ABDALAZIS *enters.*

Abdalazis. Julian, to thee, the terror of the faithless,
I bring my father's order to prepare
For the bright day that crowns thy brave exploits.
Our enemy is at the very gate,
And art thou here, with women in thy train,
Crouching to gain admittance to their lord,
And mourning the unkindness of delay !
    Julian (agitated, goes toward the door, and returns).
    I am prepared : Prince, judge not hastily.
    Abdalazis. Whether I should not promise all they ask,
I too could hesitate, though earlier taught
The duty to obey, and should rejoice
To shelter in the universal storm
A frame so delicate, so full of fears,
So little used to outrage and to arms,
As one of these, so humble, so uncheer'd
At the gay pomp that smooths the track of war.
When she beheld me from afar dismount,
And heard my trumpet, she alone drew back,
And, as though doubtful of the help she seeks,
Shudder'd to see the jewels on my brow,
And turn'd her eyes away, and wept aloud.
The other stood awhile, and then advanced :
I would have spoken ; but she waved her hand
And said, " Proceed, protect us, and avenge,
And be thou worthier of the crown thou wearest."

Hopeful and happy is indeed our cause,
When the most timid of the lovely hail
Stranger and foe.

    Roderigo (unnoticed by Abdalazis). And shrink but
        to advance.

    Abdalazis. Thou tremblest? whence, O Julian!
        whence this change?
Thou lovest still thy country.

    Julian.   Abdalazis!
All men with human feelings love their country.
Not the high-born or wealthy man alone,
Who looks upon his children, each one led
By its gay handmaid from the high alcove,
And hears them once a-day; not only he
Who hath forgotten, when his guest inquires
The name of some far village all his own;
Whose rivers bound the province, and whose hills
Touch the last cloud upon the level sky:
No; better men still better love their country.
'Tis the old mansion of their earliest friends,
The chapel of their first and best devotions.
When violence or perfidy invades,
Or when unworthy lords hold wassail there,
And wiser heads are drooping round its moats,
At last they fix their steady and stiff eye
There, there alone, stand while the trumpet blows,
And view the hostile flames above its towers
Spire, with a bitter and severe delight.

    Abdalazis (taking his hand). Thou feelest what thou
        speakest, and thy Spain

Will ne'er be shelter'd from her fate by thee.
We, whom the Prophet sends o'er many lands,
Love none above another ; Heaven assigns
Their fields and harvests to our valiant swords,
And 'tis enough : we love while we enjoy.
Whence is the man in that fantastic guise ?
Suppliant ? or herald ? he who stalks about,
And once was even seated while we spoke :
For never came he with us o'er the sea.
　　Julian. He comes as herald.
　　Roderigo.　　　　　Thou shalt know full soon,
Insulting Moor !
　　Abdalazis. He ill endures the grief
His country suffers : I will pardon him.
He lost his courage first, and then his mind ;
His courage rushes back, his mind yet wanders.
The guest of heaven was piteous to these men,
And princes stoop to feed them in their courts.

FIRST ACT : FIFTH SCENE.

RODERIGO *is going :* MUZA *enters with* EGILONA :
RODERIGO *starts back.*

　　Muza (*sternly to* EGILONA). Enter, since 'tis the
　　custom in this land.
　　Egilona (*passing* MUZA, *points to* ABDALAZIS). Is
　　this our future monarch, or art thou ?
　　Julian. 'Tis Abdalazis, son of Muza, prince
Commanding Africa, from Abyla
To where Tunisian pilots bend the eye

O'er ruin'd temples in the glassy wave.
Till quiet times and ancient laws return
He comes to govern here.
    Roderigo.   To-morrow's dawn
Proves that.
    Muza.   What art thou?
    Roderigo (drawing his sword). King.
    Abdalazis.   Amazement!
    Muza.   Treason!
    Egilona. O horror!
    Muza.   Seize him.
    Egilona.   Spare him! fly to me!
    Julian. Urge me not to protect a guest, a herald,
The blasts of war roar over him unfelt.
    Egilona. Ah fly, unhappy!
    Roderigo.   Fly! no, Egilona!
Dost thou forgive me? dost thou love me? still?
    Egilona. I hate, abominate, abhor thee—go,
Or my own vengeance——
    RODERIGO *(takes* JULIAN'S *hand; invites him to
        attack* MUZA *and* ABDALAZIS). Julian!
    Julian.   Hence, or die.

SECOND ACT: FIRST SCENE.

Camp of JULIAN.

JULIAN *and* COVILLA.

    Julian. Obdurate? I am not as I appear.
Weep, my beloved child! Covilla, weep

Into my bosom; every drop be mine
Of this most bitter soul-empoisoning cup:
Into no other bosom than thy father's
Canst thou or wouldst thou pour it.
    Covilla.   Cease, my lord,
My father, angel of my youth, when all
Was innocence and peace.
    Julian.   Arise, my love,
Look up to heaven . . . where else are souls like
      thine!
Mingle in sweet communion with its children,
Trust in its providence, its retribution,
And I will cease to mourn; for, O my child,
These tears corrode, but thine assuage, the heart.
    Covilla. And never shall I see my mother too,
My own, my blessed mother?
    Julian.   Thou shalt see
Her and thy brothers.
    Covilla.   No! I cannot look
On them, I cannot meet their lovely eyes,
I cannot lift mine up from under theirs.
We all were children when they went away;
They now have fought hard battles, and are men,
And camps and kings they know, and woes and crimes.
Sir, will they never venture from the walls
Into the plain? Remember, they are young,
Hardy and emulous and hazardous,
And who is left to guard them in the town?
    Julian. Peace is throughout the land: the various
      tribes

Of that vast region sink at once to rest,
Like one wide wood when every wind lies husht.
   Covilla. And war, in all its fury, roams o'er Spain !
   Julian. Alas ! and will for ages : crimes are loose
At which ensanguined War stands shuddering,
And calls for vengeance from the powers above,
Impatient of inflicting it himself.
Nature in these new horrors is aghast
At her own progeny, and knows them not.
I am the minister of wrath ; the hands
That tremble at me shall applaud me too,
And seal their condemnation.
   Covilla.   O kind father,
Pursue the guilty, but remember Spain.
   Julian. Child, thou wert in thy nursery short time
      since,
And latterly hast past the vacant hour
Where the familiar voice of history
Is hardly known, however nigh, attuned
In softer accents to the sickened ear ;
But thou hast heard, for nurses tell these tales,
Whether I drew my sword for Witiza
Abandoned by the people he betrayed,
Tho'·brother to the woman who of all
Was ever dearest to this broken heart,
Till thou, my daughter, wert a prey to grief,
And a brave country brookt the wrongs I bore.
For I had seen Rusilla guide the steps
Of her Theodofred, when burning brass
Plunged its fierce fang into the fount of light,

And Witiza's the guilt! when, bent with age,
He knew the voice again, and told the name
Of those whose proffer'd fortunes had been laid
Before his throne, while happiness was there,
And strain'd the sightless nerve tow'rd where they
    stood,
At the forçed memory of the very oaths
He heard renew'd from each, but heard afar,
For they were loud, and him the throng spurn'd off.
    Covilla. Who were all these?
    Julian.   All who are seen to-day
On prancing steeds richly caparisoned
In loyal acclamation round Roderigo;
Their sons beside them, loving one another
Unfeignedly, thro' joy, while they themselves
In mutual homage mutual scorn suppress.
Their very walls and roofs are welcoming
The king's approach, their storied tapestry
Swells its rich arch for him triumphantly
At every clarion blowing from below.
    Covilla. Such wicked men will never leave his side.
    Julian. For they are insects which see naught
    beyond
Where they now crawl; whose changes are complete,
Unless of habitation.
    Covilla.   Whither go
Creatures unfit for better or for wcrse?
    Julian. Some to the grave, where peace be with
    them! some
Across the Pyrenean mountains far,

Into the plains of France ; suspicion there
Will hang on every step from rich and poor,
Grey quickly-glancing eyes will wrinkle round
And courtesy will watch them, day and night.
Shameless they are, yet will they blush amid
A nation that ne'er blushes : some will drag
The captive's chain, repair the shatter'd bark,
Or heave it from a quicksand to the shore
Among the marbles of the Lybian coast,
Teach patience to the lion in his cage,
And, by the order of a higher slave,
Hold to the elephant their scanty fare
To please the children while the parent sleeps.

   Covilla. Spaniards ? must they, dear father, lead
     such lives ?
   Julian. All are not Spaniards who draw breath in
     Spain,
Those are, who live for her, who die for her,
Who love her glory and lament her fall.
O may I too——
   Covilla.   But peacefully, and late,
Live and die here !
   Julian.   I have, alas ! myself
Laid waste the hopes where my fond fancy stray'd,
And view their ruins with unalter'd eyes.
   Covilla. My mother will at last return to you.
Might I once more, but—could I now ? behold her.
Tell her—ah me ! what was my rash desire?
No, never tell her these inhuman things,
For they would waste her tender heart away

As they waste mine; or tell when I have died,
Only to show her that her every care
Could not have saved, could not have comforted;
That she herself, clasping me once again
To her sad breast, had said, Covilla! go,
Go, hide them in the bosom of thy God!
Sweet mother! that far-distant voice I hear,
And, passing out of youth and out of life,
I would not turn at last, and disobey.

SECOND ACT: SECOND SCENE.

SISABERT *enters.*

Sisabert. Uncle, and is it true, say, can it be,
That thou art leader of these faithless Moors?
That thou impeachest thy own daughter's fame
Thro' the whole land, to seize upon the throne
By the permission of these recreant slaves?
What shall I call thee? art thou, speak Count Julian,
A father, or a soldier, or a man?
    Julian. All, or this day had never seen me here.
    Sisabert. O falsehood! worse than woman's!
    Covilla.   Once, my cousin,
Far gentler words were utter'd from your lips.
If you loved me, you loved my father first,
More justly and more steadily, ere love
Was passion and illusion and deceit.
    Sisabert. I boast not that I never was deceived,
Covilla, which beyond all boasts were base,

Nor that I never loved ; let this be thine.
Illusions ! just to stop us, not delay,
Amuse, not occupy ! Too true ! when love
Scatters its brilliant foam, and passes on
To some fresh object in its natural course,
Widely and openly and wanderingly,
'Tis better : narrow it, and it pours its gloom
In one fierce cataract that stuns the soul.
Ye hate the wretch ye make so, while ye choose
Whoever knows you best and shuns you most.
　　Covilla. Shun *me* then : be beloved more and
　　more.
Honour the hand that show'd you honour first,
Love—O my father ! speak, proceed, persuade,
Your voice alone can utter it—another.
　　Sisabert. Ah, lost Covilla ! can a thirst of power
Alter thy heart thus to abandon mine,
And change my very nature at one blow?
　　Covilla. I told you, dearest Sisabert, 'twas vain
To urge me more, to question or confute.
　　Sisabert. I know it, for another wears the crown
Of Witiza my father ; who succeeds
To king Roderigo will succeed to me.
Yet thy cold perfidy still calls me dear,
And o'er my aching temples breathes one gale
Of days departed to return no more.
　　Julian. Young man, avenge our cause.
　　Sisabert.　　　　　　　　　What cause avenge ?
　　Covilla. If I was ever dear to you, hear me,
Not vengeance ; heaven will give that signal soon

O Sisabert, the pangs I have endured
On your long absence——
   Sisabert.   Will be now consoled.
Thy father comes to mount my father's throne;
But though I would not a usurper king,
I prize his valour and defend his crown :
No stranger and no traitor rules o'er me,
Or unchastised inveigles humble Spain.
Covilla, gavest thou no promises?
Nor thou, Don Julian? Seek not to reply,
Too well I know, too justly I despise,
Thy false excuse, thy coward effrontery;
Yes, when thou gavest them across the sea,
An enemy wert thou to Mahomet,
And no appellant to his faith or leagues.
  Julian. 'Tis well: a soldier hears throughout in
    silence.
I urge no answer : to those words, I fear,
Thy heart with sharp compunction will reply.
  Sisabert (to COVILLA). Then I demand of thee,
    before thou reign,
Answer me—while I fought against the Frank
Who dared to sue thee? blazon'd in the court,
Not trailed thro' darkness, were our nuptial bands ;
No; Egilona join'd our hands herself,
The peers applauded and the king approved.
  Julian. Hast thou yet seen that king since thy
    return ?
  Covilla. Father ! O Father !
  Sisabert.   I will not implore

Of him or thee what I have lost for ever.
These were not, when we parted, thy alarms ;
Far other, and far worthier of thy heart
Were they, which Sisabert could banish then.
Fear me not now, Covilla ! thou hast changed,
I am changed too.   I lived but where thou livedst,
My very life was portion'd off from thine :
Upon the surface of thy happiness
Day after day I gazed, I doted, there
Was all I had, was all I coveted ;
So pure, serene, and boundless it appear'd:
Yet, for we told each other every thought,
Thou knowest well, if thou rememberest,
At times I fear'd ; as tho' some demon sent
Suspicion without form into the world,
To whisper unimaginable things.   -
Then thy fond arguing banisht all but hope,
Each wish and every feeling was with thine,
Till I partook thy nature, and became
Credulous and incredulous like thee.
We, who have met so alter'd, meet no more.
Mountains and seas ! ye are not separation :
Death ! thou dividest, but unitest too
In everlasting peace and faith sincere.
Confiding love ! where is thy resting-place?
Where is thy truth, Covilla? where?—Go, go —
I should believe thee and adore thee still.

                                        [*Goes.*

  Covilla. O Heaven ! support me, or desert me
      quite,

And leave me lifeless this too trying hour !
He thinks me faithless.
    Julian.   He must think thee so.
    Covilla. O tell him, tell him all, when I am
        dead—
He will die too, and we shall meet again.
He will know all when these sad eyes are closed.
Ah, cannot he before? must I appear
The vilest—O just Heaven ! can it be thus?
I am—all earth resounds it—lost, despised,
Anguish and shame unutterable seize me.
'Tis palpable, no phantom, no delusion,
No dream that wakens with o'erwhelming horror ;
Spaniard and Moor fight on this ground alone,
And tear the arrow from my bleeding breast
To pierce my father's, for alike they fear.
    Julian. Invulnerable, unassailable
Are we, alone perhaps of human kind,
Nor life allures us more nor death alarms.
    Covilla. Fallen, unpitied, unbelieved, unheard !
I should have died long earlier.   Gracious God !
Desert me to my sufferings, but sustain
My faith in thee !   O hide me from the world,
And from yourself, my father, from your fondness,
That opened in this wilderness of woe
A source of tears—it else had burst my heart,
Setting me free for ever : then perhaps
A cruel war had not divided Spain,
Had not o'erturn'd her cities and her altars,
Had not endanger'd you !   O haste afar

Ere the last dreadful conflict that decides
Whether we live beneath a foreign sway——
    Julian. Or under him whose tyranny brought down
The curse upon his people. O child! child!
Urge me no further, talk not of the war,
Remember not our country.
    Covilla.   Not remember!
What have the wretched else for consolation?
What else have they who pining feed their woe?
Can I, or should I, drive from memory
All that was dear and sacred? all the joys
Of innocence and peace? when no debate
Was in the convent, but what hymn, whose voice,
To whom among the blessed it arose,
Swelling so sweet; when rang the vesper-bell
And every finger ceast from the guitar,
And every tongue was silent through our land;
When, from remotest earth, friends met again,
Hung on each other's neck, and but embraced,
So sacred, still, and peaceful was the hour.
Now, in what climate of the wasted world,
Not unmolested long by the profane,
Can I pour forth in secrecy to God
My prayers and my repentance? where beside
Is the last solace of the parting soul?
Friends, brethren, parents, dear indeed, too dear
Are they, but somewhat yet the heart requires,
That it may leave them lighter and more blest.
    Julian. Wide are the regions of our far-famed land:
Thou shalt arrive at her remotest bounds,

See her best people, choose some holiest house;
Whether where Castro from surrounding vines
Hears the hoarse ocean roar among his caves,
And, thro' the fissure in the green churchyard,
The wind wail loud the calmest summer day;
Or where Santona leans against the hill,
Hidden from sea and land by groves and bowers.

    Covilla. O ! for one moment in those pleasant
        scenes
Thou placest me, and lighter air I breathe:
Why could I not have rested, and heard on !
My voice dissolves the vision quite away,
Outcast from virtue, and from nature too !

    Julian. Nature and virtue ! they shall perish first.
God destined them for thee, and thee for them,
Inseparably and eternally !
The wisest and the best will prize thee most,
And solitudes and cities will contend
Which shall receive thee kindliest.   Sigh not so:
Violence and fraud will never penetrate
Where piety and poverty retire,
Intractable to them and valueless,
And lookt at idly like the face of heaven.
If strength be wanted for security,
Mountains the guard, forbidding all approach
With iron-pointed and uplifted gates,
Thou wilt be welcome too in Aguilar,
Impenetrable, marble-turreted,
Surveying from aloft the limpid ford,
The massive fane, the sylvan avenue;

Whose hospitality I proved myself,
A willing leader in no impious war
When fame and freedom urged me ; or mayst dwell
In Reÿnosa's dry and thriftless dale,
Unharvested beneath October moons,
Among those frank and cordial villagers.
They never saw us, and, poor simple souls !
So little know they whom they call the great,
Would pity one another less than us,
In injury, disaster, or distress.
    Covilla. But they would ask each other whence our
        grief,
That they might pity.
    Julian.   Rest then just beyond,
In the secluded scenes where Ebro springs
And drives not from his fount the fallen leaf,
So motionless and tranquil its repose.
    Covilla. Thither let us depart, and speedily.
    Julian. I cannot go : I live not in the land
I have reduced beneath such wretchedness :
And who could leave the brave whose lives and
    fortunes
Hang on his sword ?
    Covilla.   Me thou canst leave, my father ;
Ah yes, for it is past ; too well thou seest
My life and fortunes rest not upon thee.
Long, happily—could it be gloriously !
Still mayst thou live, and save thy country still !
    Julian. Unconquerable land ! unrival'd race !
Whose bravery, too enduring, rues alike

The power and weakness of accursed kings,
How cruelly hast thou neglected me !
Forcing me from thee, never to return,
Nor in thy pangs and struggles to partake !
I hear a voice ! 'tis Egilona : come,
Recall thy courage, dear unhappy girl,
Let us away.

SECOND ACT: THIRD SCENE.

Egilona enters.

Egilona.   Remain ; I order thee.
Attend, and do thy duty : I am queen,
Unbent to degradation.
    Covilla.   I attend
Ever most humbly and most gratefully,
My too kind sovran, cousin now no more.
Could I perform but half the services
I owe her, I were happy for a time,
Or dared I show her half my love, 'twere bliss.
    Egilona. Oh ! I sink under gentleness like thine.
Thy sight is death to me ; and yet 'tis dear.
The gaudy trappings of assumptive state
Drop at the voice of nature to the earth,
Before thy feet.   I cannot force myself
To hate thee, to renounce thee ; yet—Covilla !
Yet—O distracting thought ! 'tis hard to see,
Hard to converse with, to admire, to love,

As from my soul I do, and must do, thee,
One who hath robb'd me of all pride and joy,
All dignity, all fondness.   I adored
Roderigo.   He was brave, and in discourse
Most voluble ; the masses of his mind
Were vast, but varied ; now absorb'd in gloom,
Majestic, not austere ; now their extent
Opening and waving in bright levity——
   Julian. Depart, my daughter.   'Twere as well to bear
His presence as his praise.   Go ; she will dream
This phantasm out, nor notice thee depart.
                    [COVILLA *goes.*
   Egilona. What pliancy !   what tenderness ! what life !
O for the smiles of those who smile so seldom,
The love of those who know no other love !
Such he was, Egilona, who was thine.
   Julian. While he was worthy of the realm and thee.
   Egilona. Can it be true then, Julian, that thy aim
Is sovranty ? not virtue nor revenge ?
   Julian. I swear to heaven, nor I nor child of mine
Ever shall mount to this polluted throne.
   Egilona. Then am I yet a queen.   The savage Moor
Who could not conquer Ceuta from thy sword
In his own country, not with every wile
Of his whole race, not with his myriad crests
Of cavalry, seen from the Calpian highths

Like locusts on the parcht and gleamy coast,
Will never conquer Spain.
   Julian.   Spain then was conquer'd
When fell her laws before the traitor king.

SECOND ACT: FOURTH SCENE.

Officer announces OPAS.

O queen, the metropolitan attends
On matter of high import to the state,
And wishes to confer in privacy.
   Egilona (*to* JULIAN). Adieu, then; and whate'er
       betide the country,
Sustain at least the honours of our house.
                [JULIAN *goes before* OPAS *enters.*
   Opas. I cannot but commend, O Egilona,
Such resignation and such dignity.
Indeed he is unworthy; yet a queen
Rather to look for peace, and live remote
From cities, and from courts, and from her lord,
I hardly could expect in one so young,
So early, widely, wondrously admired.
   Egilona. I am resolv'd : religious men, good Opas,
In this resemble the vain libertine ;
They find in woman no consistency,
No virtue but devotion, such as comes
To infancy or age or fear or love,
Seeking a place of rest, and finding none
Until it soar to heaven.

Opas.   A spring of mind
That rises when all pressure is removed,
Firmness in pious and in chaste resolves,
But weakness in much fondness ; these, O queen,
I did expect, I own.
   Egilona.   The better part
Be mine ; the worse hath been, and is no more.
   Opas. But if Roderigo have at length prevail'd
That Egilona willingly resigns
All claim to royalty, and casts away,
Indifferent or estranged, the marriage-bond
His perjury tore asunder, still the church
Hardly can sanction his new nuptial rites.
   Egilona. What art thou saying? what new nuptial
     rites ?
   Opas. Thou knowest not ?
   Egilona.   Am I a wife ? a queen ?
Abandon it ! my claim to royalty !
Whose hand was on my head when I arose
Queen of this land ? whose benediction sealed
My marriage-vow ? who broke it? was it I ?
And wouldst thou, virtuous Opas, wouldst thou dim
The glorious light of thy declining days ?
Wouldst thou administer the sacred vows
And sanction them, and bless them, for another,
And bid her live in peace while I am living ?
Go then ; I execrate and banish him
For ever from my sight : we were not born
For happiness together ; none on earth
Were ever so dissimilar as we.

He is not worth a tear, a wish, a thought;
Never was I deceived in him; I found
No tenderness, no fondness, from the first.
A love of power, a love of perfidy,
Such is the love that is return'd for mine.
Ungrateful man! 'twas not the pageantry
Of regal state, the clarions, nor the guard,
Nor loyal valour, nor submissive beauty,
Silence at my approach, awe at my voice,
Happiness at my smile, that led my youth
Toward Roderigo. I had lived obscure,
In humbleness, in poverty, in want,
Blest, O supremely blest, with him alone;
And he abandons me, rejects me, scorns me,
Insensible! inhuman! for another!
Thou shalt repent thy wretched choice, false man!
Crimes such as thine call loudly for perdition;
Heaven will inflict it, and not I; but I
Neither will fall alone nor live despised.

　　　　　　　　　　　　　[*A trumpet sounds.*

　Opas. Peace, Egilona! he arrives: compose
Thy turbid thoughts, meet him with dignity.
　Egilona. He! in the camp of Julian! trust me, sir,
He comes not hither, dares no longer use
The signs of state, and flies from every foe.

　　　　　　　　　　　　　[*Retires some distance.*

SECOND ACT : FIFTH SCENE.

Enter MUZA *and* ABDALAZIS.

Muza (*to* ABDALAZIS). I saw him but an instant,
　　and disguised,
Yet this is not the traitor; on his brow
Observe the calm of wisdom and of years.
　　Opas. Whom seekest thou?
　　Muza.　　　　　　　Him who was king I seek.
He came array'd as herald to this tent.
　　Abdalazis. Thy daughter! was she nigh? perhaps
　　for her
Was this disguise.
　　Muza.　　　　　Here, Abdalazis, kings
Disguise from other causes ; they obtain
Beauty by violence, and power by raud.
Treason was his intent : we must admit
Whoever come ; our numbers are too small
For question or selection, and the blood
Of Spaniards shall win Spain for us to-day.
　　Abdalazis. The wicked cannot move from under-
　　neath
Thy ruling eye.
　　Muza.　　　　Right ! Julian and Roderigo
Are leagued against us, on these terms alone,
That Julian's daughter weds the christian king.
　　Egilona (*rushing forward*). 'Tis true—and I pro-
　　claim it.
　　Abdalazis.　　　　　　　Heaven and earth !

Was it not thou, most lovely, most high-souled,
Who wishedst us success, and me a crown?
                        [OPAS *goes abruptly*
   Egilona. I give it—I am Egilona, queen
Of that detested man.
   Abdalazis.   I touch the hand
That chains down fortune to the throne of fate,
And will avenge thee; for 'twas thy command,
'Tis Heaven's. My father! what retards our bliss?
Why art thou silent?
   Muza.   Inexperienced years
Rather would rest on the soft lap, I see,
Of pleasure, after the fierce gusts of war.
O destiny! that callest me alone,
Hapless, to keep the toilsome watch of state,
Painful to age, unnatural to youth,
Adverse to all society of friends,
Equality, and liberty, and ease,
The welcome cheer of the unbidden feast,
The gay reply, light, sudden, like the leap
Of the young forester's unbended bow,
But, above all, to tenderness at home,
And sweet security of kind concern
Even from those who seem most truly ours.
Who would resign all this, to be approacht,
Like a sick infant by a canting nurse,
To spread his arms in darkness, and to find
One universal hollowness. around?
Forego a little while that bane of peace:
Love may be cherisht.

Abdalazis.   'Tis enough ; I ask
No other boon.
    Muza.   Not victory ?
    Abdalazis.   Farewell,
O queen ! I will deserve thee ; why do tears
Silently drop, and slowly, down thy veil ?
I shall return to worship thee, and soon ;
Why this affliction ? O, that I alone
Could raise or could repress it !
    Egilona.   We depart,
Nor interrupt your counsels, nor impede ;
O may they prosper, whatsoe'er they be,
And perfidy soon meet its just reward !
The infirm and peaceful Opas—whither gone ?
    Muza. Stay, daughter ; not for counsel are we met,
But to secure our arms from treachery,
O'erthrow and stifle base conspiracies,
Involve in his own toils our false ally——
    Egilona. Author of every woe I have endured !
Ah, sacrilegious man ! he vowed to heaven
None of his blood should ever mount the throne.
    Muza. Herein his vow indeed is ratified ;
Yet faithful ears have heard this offer made,
And weighty was the conference that ensued,
And long, not dubious ; for what mortal e'er
Refused alliance with illustrious power,
Though some have given its enjoyments up,
Tired and enfeebled by satiety ?
His friends and partisans, 'twas his pretence,
Should pass uninterrupted ; hence his camp

Is open every day to enemies.
You look around, O queen, as though you fear'd
Their entrance. Julian I pursue no more ;
You conquer him. Return we. I bequeath
Ruin, extermination, not reproach.
How we may best attain your peace and will
We must consider in some other place,
Not, lady, in the midst of snares and wiles
How to supplant your charms and seize your crown.
I rescue it ; fear not. Yes, we retire.
Whatever is your wish becomes my own,
Nor is there in this land but who obeys.

                      [He leads her away.

THIRD ACT : FIRST SCENE.

Palace in Xeres.

RODERIGO *and* OPAS.

Roderigo. Impossible ! she could not thus resign
Me for a miscreant of Barbary,
A mere adventurer; but that citron face
Shall bleach and shrivel the whole winter long,
There on yon cork-tree by the sallyport.
She shall return.
    Opas.   To fondness and to faith ?
Dost thou retain them, if she could return ?
    Roderigo. Retain them ? she has forfeited by this
All right to fondness, all to royalty.
    Opas. Consider and speak calmly : she deserves
Some pity, some reproof.

Roderigo.   To speak then calmly,
Since thine eyes open and can see her guilt—
Infamous and atrocious ! let her go—
Chains——
    Opas.   What ! in Muza's camp ?
    Roderigo.   My scorn supreme !
    Opas. Say pity.
    Roderigo.   Ay, ay, pity : that suits best.
I loved her, but *had* loved her ; three whole years
Of pleasure, and of varied pleasure too,
Had worn the soft impression half away.
What I once felt, I would recall; the faint
Responsive voice grew fainter each reply:
Imagination sank amid the scenes
It labour'd to create : the vivid joy
Of fleeting youth I follow'd and possest.
'Tis the first moment of the tenderest hour,
'Tis the first mien on entering new delights,
We give our peace, our power, our souls, for these.
    Opas. Thou hast ; and what remains ?
    Roderigo.   Roderigo : one
Whom hatred cannot reach nor love cast down.
    Opas. Nor gratitude nor pity nor remorse
Call back, nor vows nor earth nor heaven controul.
But art thou free and happy ? art thou safe ?
By shrewd contempt the humblest may chastise
Whom scarlet and its ermine cannot scare,
And the sword skulks for everywhere in vain.
Thee the poor victim of thy outrages,
Woman, with all her weakness, may despise.

Roderigo. But first let quiet age have intervened.

Opas. Ne'er will the peace or apathy of age
Be thine, or twilight steal upon thy day.
The violent choose, but cannot change, their end ;
Violence, by man or nature, must be theirs ;
Thine it must be; and who to pity thee ?

Roderigo. Behold my solace ! none.   I want no
    pity.

Opas. Proclaim we those the happiest of mankind
Who never knew a want ?   O what a curse
To thee this utter ignorance of thine !
Julian, whom all the good commiserate,
Sees thee below him far in happiness.
A state indeed of no quick restlessness,
No glancing agitation, one vast swell
Of melancholy, deep, impassable,
Interminable, where his spirit alone
Broods and o'ershadows all, bears him from earth,
And purifies his chasten'd soul for heaven.
Both heaven and earth shall from thy grasp recede.
Whether on death or life thou arguest,
Untutor'd savage or corrupted heathen
Avows no sentiment so vile as thine.

Roderigo. Nor feels ?

Opas.   O human nature ! I have heard
The secrets of the soul, and pitied thee.
Bad and accursed things have men confess'd
Before me, but have left them unarrayed,
Naked, and shivering with deformity.
The troubled dreams and deafening gush of youth

Fling o'er the fancy, struggling to be free,
Discordant and impracticable things :
If the good shudder at their past escapes,
Shall not the wicked shudder at their crimes ?
They shall : and I denounce upon thy head
God's vengeance : thou shalt rule this land no more.
    Roderigo. What ! my own kindred leave me and
      renounce me !
    Opas. Kindred? and is there any in our world
So near us as those sources of all joy,
Those on whose bosom every gale of life
Blows softly, who reflect our images
In loveliness through sorrows and through age,
And bear them onward far beyond the grave ?
    Roderigo. Methinks, most reverend Opas, not inapt
Are these fair views ; arise they from Seville ?
    Opas. He who can scoff at them may scoff at me.
Such are we, that the Giver of all Good
Shall, in the heart he purifies, possess
The latest love; the earliest, no, not there !
I've known the firm and faithful: even from them
Life's eddying spring shed the first bloom on earth.
I pity them, but ask their pity too :
I love the happiness of men, and praise
And sanctify the blessings I renounce.
    Roderigo. Yet would thy baleful influence under-
      mine
The heaven-appointed throne.
    Opas.   The throne of guilt
Obdurate, without plea, without remorse.

Roderigo. What power hast thou ? perhaps thou
   soon wilt want
A place of refuge.
   Opas.   Rather say, perhaps
My place of refuge will receive me soon.
Could I extend it even to thy crimes,
It should be open ; but the wrath of heaven
Turns them against thee and subverts thy sway :
It leaves thee not, what wickedness and woe
Oft in their drear communion taste together,
Hope and repentance.
   Roderigo.   But it leaves me arms,
Vigour of soul and body, and a race
Subject by law and dutiful by choice,
Whose hand is never to be holden fast
Within the closing cleft of gnarled creeds;
No easy prey for these vile mitred Moors.
I, who received thy homage, may retort
Thy threats, vain prelate, and abase thy pride.
   Opas. Low must be those whom mortal can sink
   lower,
Nor high are they whom human power may raise.
   Roderigo. Judge now: for hear the signal.
   Opas.   And derides
Thy buoyant heart the dubious gulphs of war ?
Trumpets may sound, and not to victory.   [power.
   Roderigo. The traitor and his daughter feel my
   Opas. Just God ! avert it !
   Roderigo.   Seize this rebel priest.
I will alone subdue my enemies.   [*Goes out.*

THIRD ACT: SECOND SCENE.

RAMIRO *and* OSMA *enter from opposite sides.*

Ramiro. Where is the king? his car is at the gate,
His ministers attend him, but his foes
Are yet more prompt, nor will await delay.
   Osma. Nor need they, for he meets them as I
     speak.
Ramiro. With all his forces? or our cause is lost.
Julian and Sisabert surround the walls.
   Osma. Surround, sayst thou? enter they not the
     gates?
   Ramiro. Perhaps ere now they enter.
   Osma.   Sisabert
Brings him our prisoner.
   Ramiro.   They are friends! they held
A parley; and the soldiers, when they saw
Count Julian, lower'd their arms and hail'd him king.
   Osma. How? and he leads them in the name of
     king?
   Ramiro. He leads them; but amid that acclama-
     tion
He turn'd away his head, and call'd for vengeance.
   Osma. In Sisabert, and in the cavalry
He led, were all our hopes.
   Opas.   Woe, woe is theirs
Who have no other.
   Osma.   What are thine? obey
The just commands of our offended king:

Conduct him to the tower—off—instantly.

               [Guard *hesitates :* OPAS *goes.*

Ramiro, let us haste to reinforce——

   Ramiro. Hark ! is the king defeated? hark !

   Osma.   I hear

Such acclamation as from victory

Arises not, but rather from revolt,

Reiterated, interrupted, lost.

Favour like this his genius will retrieve

By time or promises or chastisement,

Whiche'er he choose ; the speediest is the best.

His danger and his glory let us share ;

'Tis ours to serve him.

   Ramiro.   While he rules 'tis ours.

What chariot-wheels are thundering o'er the bridge?

   Osma. Roderigo's ; I well know them.

   Ramiro.   Now, the burst

Of acclamation ! now ! again, again.

   Osma. I know the voices ; they are for Roderigo.

   Ramiro. Stay, I entreat thee. One hath now
      prevail'd.

So far is certain.

   Osma.   Ay, the right prevails.

   Ramiro. Transient and vain their joyance who
      rejoice

Precipitately and intemperately,

And bitter thoughts grow up where'er it fell.

   Osma. Nor vain and transient theirs who idly float

Down popularity's unfertile stream,

And fancy all their own that rises round.

                            599

Ramiro. If thou yet lovest, as I know thou dost,
Thy king——
    Osma.   I love him ; for he owes me much,
Brave soul ! and cannot, though he would, repay.
Service and faith, pure faith and service hard,
Throughout his reign, if these things be desert,
These have I borne toward him, and still bear.
    Ramiro. Come, from thy solitary eyrie come,
And share the prey, so plenteous and profuse,
Which a less valorous brood will else consume.
Much fruit is shaken down in civil storms:
And shall not orderly and loyal hands
Gather it up? (*Loud shouts.*)   Again ! and   yet
    refuse ?
How different are those citizens without
From thee ! from thy serenity ! thy arch,
Thy firmament, of intrepidity !
For their new lord, whom they have never served,
Afraid were they to shout, and only struck
The pavement with their ferrels and their feet :
Now they are certain of the great event
Voices and hands they raise, and all contend
Who shall be bravest in applauding most.
Knowest thou these ?
    Osma.   Their voices I know well—
And can they shout for him they would have slain ?
A prince untried they welcome ; soon their doubts
Are blown afar.
    Ramiro.   Yes, brighter scenes arise.
The disunited he alone unites,

The weak with hope he strengthens, and the strong
With justice.
    Osma.   Wait : praise him when time hath given
A soundness and consistency to praise :
He shares it amply who bestows it right.
    Ramiro. Doubtless thou?
    Osma.   Be it so : let us away ;
New courtiers come.
    Ramiro.   And why not join the new ?
Let us attend him and congratulate ;
Come on ; they enter.
    Osma.   This is now my post
No longer : I could face them in the field,
I cannot here.
    Ramiro.   To-morrow all may change ;
Be comforted.
    Osma.   I want nor change nor comfort.
    Ramiro. The prisoner's voice !
    Osma.   The metropolitan's ?
Triumph he may—not over me forgiven.
This way, and thro' the chapel : none are there.
                       [Goes out.

THIRD ACT : THIRD SCENE.

OPAS *and* SISABERT.

Opas. The royal threats still sound along these
    halls :
Hardly his foot hath past them, and he flees

From his own treachery; all his pride, his hopes,
Are scatter'd at a breath; even courage fails
Now falsehood sinks from under him.   Behold,
Again art thou where reign'd thy ancestors;
Behold the chapel of thy earliest prayers,
Where I, whose chains are sunder'd at thy sight
Ere they could close around these aged limbs,
Received and blest thee, when thy mother's arm
Was doubtful if it loost thee ! with delight
Have I observed the promises we made
Deeply imprest and manfully perform'd.
Now, to thyself beneficent. O prince,
Never henceforth renew those weak complaints
Against Covilla's vows and Julian's faith,
His honour broken, and her heart estranged.
O, if thou holdest peace or glory dear,
Away with jealousy ; brave Sisabert,
Smite from thy bosom, smite that scorpion down :
It swells and hardens amid mildew'd hopes,
O'erspreads and blackens whate'er most delights,
And renders us, haters of loveliness,
The lowest of the fiends : ambition led
The higher on, furious to dispossess,
From admiration sprung and frenzied love.
This disingenuous soul-debasing passion,
Rising from abject and most sordid fear,
Consumes the vitals, pines, and never dies.
For Julian's truth have I not pledged my own ?
Have I not sworn Covilla weds no other ?
    Sisabert. Her persecutor have not I chastised ?

Have not I fought for Julian, won the town, and
    liberated thee?
   Opas.   But left for him
The dangers of pursuit, of ambuscade,
Of absence from thy high and splendid name.
   Sisabert. Do probity and truth want such sup-
    ports?
   Opas. Gryphens and eagles, ivory and gold,
Can add no clearness to the lamp above,
But many look for them in palaces
Who have them not, and want them not, at home.
Virtue and valour and experience
Are never trusted by themselves alone
Further than infancy and idiocy:
The men around him, not the man himself,
Are lookt at, and by these is he preferr'd.
'Tis the green mantle of the warrener
And his loud whistle that alone attract
The lofty gazes of the noble herd:
And thus, without thy countenance and help,
Feeble and faint is yet our confidence,
Brief perhaps our success.
   Sisabert.   Should I resign
To Abdalazis her I once adored?
He truly, he must wed a Spanish queen!
He rule in Spain! ah! whom could any land
Obey so gladly as the meek, the humble,
The friend of all who have no friend beside,
Covilla! could he choose or could he find
Another who might so confirm his power?

And now indeed from long domestic wars
Who else survives of all our ancient house?
   Opas. But Egilona.
   Sisabert.   Vainly she upbraids
Roderigo.
   Opas.   She divorces him, abjures,
And carries vengeance to that hideous highth
Which piety and chastity would shrink
To look from, on the world or on themselves.
   Sisabert. She may forgive him yet.
   Opas.   Ah, Sisabert !
Wretched are those a woman has forgiven :
With her forgiveness ne'er hath love return'd.
Ye know not till too late the filmy tie
That holds heaven's precious boon eternally
To such as fondly cherish her ; once go
Driven by mad passion, strike but at her peace,
And, though she step aside from broad reproach,
Yet every softer virtue dies away.
Beaming with virtue inaccessible
Stood Egilona ; for her lord she lived,
And for the heavens that raised her sphere so high :
All thoughts were on her, all, beside her own.
Negligent as the blossoms of the field,
Array'd in candour and simplicity,
Before her path she heard the streams of joy
Murmur her name in all their cadences,
Saw them in every scene, in light, in shade,
Reflect her image, but acknowledge them
Hers most complete when flowing from her most.

All things in want of her, herself of none,
Pomp and dominion lay beneath her feet
Unfelt and unregarded. Now behold
The earthly passions war against the heavenly !
Pride against love, ambition and revenge
Against devotion and compliancy:
Her glorious beams adversity hath blunted;
And coming nearer to our quiet view,
The original clay of coarse mortality
Hardens and flaws around her.
　　Sisabert.　　　　　　　　　　　Every germ
Of virtue perishes when love recedes
From those hot shifting sands, the female heart.
　　Opas. His was the fault; be his the punishment.
'Tis not their own crimes only men commit,
They harrow them into another's breast,
And they shall reap the bitter growth with pain.
　　Sisabert. Yes, blooming royalty will first attract
These creatures of the desert.　Now I breathe
More freely.　She is theirs if I pursue
The fugitive again.　He well deserves
The death he flies from.　Stay !　Don Julian twice
Call'd him aloud, and he, methinks, replied.
Could not I have remain'd a moment more
And seen the end ? although with hurried voice
He bade me intercept the scattered foes,
And hold the city barr'd to their return.
May Egilona be another's wife
Whether he die or live ! but oh ! Covilla !
She never can be mine ! yet she may be

Still happy—no, Covilla, no—not happy,
But more deserving happiness without it.
Mine never ! nor another's. 'Tis enough.
The tears I shed no rival can deride ;
In the fond intercourse a name once cherisht
Will never be defended by faint smiles,
Nor given up with vows of alter'd love.
And is the passion of my soul at last
Reduced to this ? is this my happiness ?
This my sole comfort ? this the close of all
Those promises, those tears, those last adieus,
And those long vigils for the morrow's dawn ?
    Opas. Arouse thee ! be thyself.   O Sisabert,
Awake to glory from these feverish dreams :
The enemy is in our land ; two enemies ;
We must quell both : shame on us if we fail.
    Sisabert. Incredible ! a nation be subdued
Peopled as ours.
    Opas.   Corruption may subvert
What force could never.
    Sisabert.   Traitors may.
    Opas.   Alas !
If traitors can, the basis is but frail.
I mean such traitors as the vacant world
Echoes most stunningly : not fur-robed knaves
Whose whispers raise the dreaming bloodhound's ear
Against benighted famisht wanderers,
While with remorseless guilt they undermine
Palace and shed, their very father's house.
O blind ! their own, their children's heritage,

To leave more ample space for fearful wealth.
Plunder in some most harmless guise they swathe,
Call it some very meek and hallow'd name,
Some known and borne by their good forefathers,
And own and vaunt it thus redeem'd from sin.
These are the plagues heaven sends o'er every land
Before it sink—the portents of the street,
Not of the air—lest nations should complain
Of distance or of dimness in the signs,
Flaring from far to Wisdom's eye alone:
These are the last : these, when the sun rides high
In the forenoon of doomsday, revelling,
Make men abhor the earth, arraign the skies.
Ye who behold them spoil field after field,
Despising them in individual strength,
Not with one torrent sweeping them away
Into the ocean of eternity,
Arise ! despatch ! no renovating gale,
No second spring awaits you : up, begone,
If you have force and courage even for flight.
The blast of dissolution is behind.
    Sisabert. How terrible ! how true ! what voice like
        thine
Can rouse and warn the nation !   If she rise,
Say, whither go, where stop we?
    Opas.   God will guide.
Let us pursue the oppressor to destruction ;
The rest is Heaven's : must we move no step
Because we cannot see the boundaries
Of our long way, and every stone between ?

Sisabert. Is not thy vengeance for the late affront,
For threats and outrage and imprisonment?
Opas. For outrage, yes; imprisonment and threats
I pardon him, and whatsoever ill
He could do *me.*
Sisabert.   To hold Covilla from me!
To urge her into vows against her faith,
Against her beauty, youth, and inclination,
Without her mother's blessing, nay, without
Her father's knowledge and authority,
So that she never will behold me more,
Flying afar for refuge and for help
Where never friend but God will comfort her!
Opas. These and more barbarous deeds were per-
          petrated.
Sisabert. Yet her proud father deign'd not to inform
Me, whom he loved and taught, in peace and war,
Me, whom he called his son, before I hoped
To merit it by marriage or by arms.
He offer'd no excuse, no plea; exprest
No sorrow; but with firm unfaltering voice
Commanded me—I trembled as he spoke—
To follow where he led, redress his wrongs,
And vindicate the honour of his child.
He call'd on God, the witness of his cause,
On Spain, the partner of his victories;
And yet amid these animating words
Roll'd the huge tear down his unvisor'd face;
A general swell of indignation rose
Thro' the long line, sobs burst from every breast,

Hardly one voice succeeded ; you might hear
The impatient hoof strike the soft sandy plain.
But when the gates flew open, and the king
In his high car came forth triumphantly,
Then was Count Julian's stature more elate ;
Tremendous was the smile that smote the eyes
Of all he past. ' *Fathers, and sons, and brothers,*'
He cried, '*I fight your battles, follow me !*
Soldiers, we know no danger but disgrace !'
'*Father, and general, and king,*' they shout,
And would proclaim him : back he cast his face,
Pallid with grief, and one loud groan burst forth ;
It kindled vengeance thro' the Asturian ranks,
And they soon scatter'd, as the blasts of heaven
Scatter the leaves and dust, the astonisht foe.
   Opas. And doubtest thou his truth ?
   Sisabert.   I love—and doubt—
Fight—and believe : Roderigo spoke untruths ;
In him I place no trust ; but Julian holds
Truths in reserve : how should I quite confide !
   Opas. By sorrows thou beholdest him opprest ;
Doubt the more prosperous. March, Sisabert,
Once more against his enemy and ours :
Much hath been done, but much there yet remains.

FOURTH ACT : FIRST SCENE.

Tent of JULIAN.

RODERIGO *and* JULIAN.

Julian. The people had deserted thee, and throng'd
My standard, had I raised it, at the first;
But once subsiding, and no voice of mine
Calling by name each grievance to each man,
They, silent and submissive by degrees,
Bore thy hard yoke, and, hadst thou but opprest,
Would still have borne it : thou hast now deceived;
Thou hast done all a foreign foe could do
And more against them; with ingratitude
Not hell itself could arm the foreign foe;
'Tis forged at home and kills not from afar.
Amid whate'er vain glories fell upon
Thy rainbow span of power, which I dissolve,
Boast not how thou conferredst wealth and rank,
How thou preservedst me, my family,
All my distinctions, all my offices,
When Witiza was murder'd; that I stand
Count Julian at this hour by special grace.
The sword of Julian saved the walls of Ceuta,
And not the shadow that attends his name :
It was no badge, no title, that o'erthrew
Soldier and steed and engine.   Don Roderigo !
The truly and the falsely great here differ :
These by dull wealth or daring fraud advance;

Him the Almighty calls amid his people
To sway the wills and passions of mankind.
The weak of heart and intellect beheld
Thy splendour, and adored thee lord of Spain:
I rose—Roderigo lords o'er Spain no more.
    Roderigo. Now to a traitor's add a boaster's name.
    Julian. Shameless and arrogant, dost thou believe
I boast for pride or pastime? forced to boast,
Truth costs me more than falsehood e'er cost thee.
Divested of that purple of the soul,
That potency, that palm of wise ambition,
Cast headlong by thy madness from that high,
That only eminence 'twixt earth and heaven,
Virtue, which some desert, but none despise,
Whether thou art beheld again on earth,
Whether a captive or a fugitive,
Miner or galley-slave, depends on me;
But he alone who made me what I am
Can make me greater or can make me less.
    Roderigo. Chance, and chance only, threw me in
        thy power;
Give me my sword again and try my strength.
    Julian. I tried it in the front of thousands.
    Roderigo.   Death
At least vouchsafe me from a soldier's hand.
    Julian. I love to hear thee ask it: now my own
Would not be bitter; no, nor immature.
    Roderigo. Defy it, say thou rather.
    Julian.   Death itself
Shall not be granted thee, unless from God;

A dole from his and from no other hand.
Thou shalt now hear and own thine infamy.
  Roderigo. Chains, dungeons, tortures—but I hear
   no more.
  Julian. Silence, thou wretch! live on—ay, live—
   abhorr'd.
Thou shalt have tortures, dungeons, chains enough;
They naturally rise and grow around
Monsters like thee, everywhere, and for ever.
  Roderigo. Insulter of the fallen! must I endure
Commands as well as threats? my vassal's too?
Nor breathe from underneath his trampling feet?
  Julian. Could I speak patiently who speak to thee,
I would say more: part of thy punishment
It should be, to be taught.
  Roderigo.   Reserve thy wisdom
 Until thy patience come, its best ally:
I learn no lore, of peace or war, from thee.
  Julian. No, thou shalt study soon another tongue,
And suns more ardent shall mature thy mind.
Either the cross thou bearest, and thy knees
Among the silent caves of Palestine
Wear the sharp flints away with midnight prayer,
Or thou shalt keep the fasts of Barbary,
Shalt wait amid the crowds that throng the well
From sultry noon till the skies fade again,
To draw up water and to bring it home
In the crackt gourd of some vile testy knave,
Who spurns thee back with bastinaded foot
For ignorance or delay of his command.

Roderigo. Rather the poison or the bowstring.
Julian.   Slaves
To other's passions die such deaths as those :
Slaves to their own should die——
   Roderigo.   What worse?
   Julian.   Their own.
   Roderigo. Is this thy counsel, renegade ?
   Julian.   Not mine :
I point a better path, nay, force thee on.
I shelter thee from every brave man's sword
While I am near thee : I bestow on thee
Life : if thou die, 'tis when thou sojournest
Protected by this arm and voice no more :
'Tis slavishly, 'tis ignominiously,
 Tis by a villain's knife.
   Roderigo.   By whose?
   Julian.   Roderigo's.
   Roderigo. O powers of vengeance ! must I hear?—
      endure ?—
Live?
   Julian. Call thy vassals : no ? then wipe the drops
Of froward childhood from thy shameless eyes.
So! thou canst weep for passion; not for pity.
   Roderigo. One hour ago I ruled all Spain ! a
      camp
Not larger than a sheepfold stood alone
Against me : now, no friend throughout the world
Follows my steps or hearkens to my call.
Behold the turns of fortune, and expect
No better : of all faithless men the Moors

Are the most faithless : from thy own experience
Thou canst not value nor rely on them.
   Julian. I value not the mass that makes my sword,
Yet while I use it I rely on it.
   Roderigo. Julian, thy gloomy soul still meditates—
Plainly I see it—death to me—pursue
The dictates of thy leaders, let revenge
Have its full sway, let Barbary prevail,
And the pure creed her elders have embraced :
Those placid sages hold assassination
A most compendious supplement to law.
   Julian. Thou knowest not the one, nor I the other.
Torn hast thou from me all my soul held dear,
Her form, her voice, all, hast thou banisht from me,
Nor dare I, wretched as I am ! recall
Those solaces of every grief erewhile.
I stand abased before insulting crime,
I falter like a criminal myself ;
The hand that hurl'd thy chariot o'er its wheels,
That held thy steeds erect and motionless
As molten statues on some palace-gate,
Shakes as with palsied age before thee now
Gone is the treasure of my heart for ever,
Without a father, mother, friend, or name.
Daughter of Julian—Such was her delight—
Such was mine too ! what pride more innocent,
What surely less deserving pangs like these,
Than springs from filial and parental love !
Debarr'd from every hope that issues forth
To meet the balmy breath of early life,

Her sadden'd days, all cold and colourless,
Will stretch before her their whole weary length
Amid the sameness of obscurity.
She wanted not seclusion to unveil
Her thoughts to heaven, cloister, nor midnight bell;
She found it in all places, at all hours:
While to assuage my labours she indulged
A playfulness that shunn'd a mother's eye,
Still to avert my perils there arose
A piety that even from *me* retired.

   Roderigo. Such was she! what am I! those are the arms
That are triumphant when the battle fails.
O Julian! Julian! all thy former words
Struck but the imbecile plumes of vanity,
These thro' its steely coverings pierce the heart.
I ask not life nor death; but, if I live,
Send my most bitter enemy to watch
My secret paths, send poverty, send pain—
I will add more—wise as thou art, thou knowest
No foe more furious than forgiven kings.
I ask not then what thou wouldst never grant:
May heaven, O Julian, from thy hand receive
A pardon'd man, a chasten'd criminal.

   Julian. This further curse hast thou inflicted; wretch!
I cannot pardon thee.

   Roderigo.   Thy tone, thy mien,
Refute those words.

   Julian.   No—I can *not* forgive.

                        600

Roderigo. Upon my knee, my conqueror, I implore !
Upon the earth, before thy feet—hard heart !
   Julian. Audacious ! hast thou never heard that
     prayer
And scorn'd it ? 'tis the last thou shouldst repeat.
Upon the earth ! upon her knees ! O God ?
   Roderigo. Resemble not a wretch so lost as I :
Be better ; O ! be happier ; and pronounce it.
   Julian. I swerve not from my purpose : thou art
     mine,
Conquer'd ; and I have sworn to dedicate,
Like a torn banner on my chapel's roof,
Thee to that power from whom thou hast rebell'd.
Expiate thy crimes by prayer, by penances.
   Roderigo. Hasten the hour of trial, speak of peace.
Pardon me not then, but with purer lips
Implore of God, who *would* hear *thee*, to pardon.
   Julian. Hope it I may—pronounce it—O Roderigo !
Ask it of him who can ; I too will ask,
And, in my own transgressions, pray for thine.
   Roderigo. One name I dare not——
   Julian.   Go ; abstain from that ;
I do conjure thee, raise not in my soul
Again the tempest that has wreckt my fame ;
Thou shalt not breathe in the same clime with her.
Far o'er the unebbing sea thou shalt adore
The eastern star, and may thy end be peace.

FOURTH ACT: SECOND SCENE.

RODERIGO *goes :* HERNANDO *enters.*

Hernando. From the prince Tarik I am sent, my
    lord.
Julian. A welcome messager, my brave Hernando.
How fares it with the gallant soul of Tarik?
    Hernando. Most joyfully; he scarcely had pro-
    nounced
Your glorious name, and bid me urge your speed,
Than, with a voice as though it answer'd heaven,
'*He shall confound them in their dark designs,*'
Cried he, and turn'd away, with that swift stride
Wherewith he meets and quells his enemies.
    Julian. Alas! I cannot bear felicitation,
Who shunn'd it even in felicity.
    Hernando. Often we hardly think ourselves the
    happy
Unless we hear it said by those around.
O my lord Julian, how your praises cheer'd
Our poor endeavours! sure, all hearts are open
Lofty and low, wise and unwise, to praise.
Even the departed spirit hovers round
Our blessings and our prayers; the corse itself
Hath shined with other light than the still stars
Shed on its rest, or the dim taper nigh.
My father, old men say who saw him dead,
And heard your lips pronounce him good and happy,

Smiled faintly through the quiet gloom that eve,
And the shroud throbb'd upon his grateful breast.
Howe'er it be, many who tell the tale
Are good and happy from that voice of praise.
His guidance and example were denied
My youth and childhood : what I am I owe——
    Julian. Hernando, look not back: a narrow path
And arduous lies before thee ; if thou stop
Thou fallest ; go right onward, nor observe
Closely and rigidly another's way,
But, free and active, follow up thy own.
    Hernando. The voice that urges now my manly step
Onward in life, recalls me to the past,
And from that fount I freshen for the goal.
Early in youth, among us villagers
Converse and ripen'd counsel you bestow'd.
O happy days of (far departed !) peace,
Days when the mighty Julian stoopt his brow
Entering our cottage-door ; another air
Breath'd through the house ; tired age and lightsome
    youth
Beheld him with intensest gaze ; these felt
More chasten'd joy ; they more profound repose.
Yes, my best lord, when labour sent them home
And mid-day suns, when from the social meal
The wicker window held the summer heat,
Prais'd have those been who, going unperceived,
Open'd it wide that all might see you well :
Nor were the children blamed, hurrying to watch
Upon the mat what rush would last arise

From your foot's pressure, ere the door was closed,
And not yet wondering how they dared to love.
Your counsels are more precious now than ever,
But are they—pardon if I err—the same ?
Tarik is gallant, kind, the friend of Julian,
Can he be more ? or ought he to be less ?
Alas ! his faith !

    Julian.   In peace or war ? Hernando.

    Hernando. O, neither ; far above it ; faith in God.

    Julian. 'Tis God's, not thine : embrace it not, nor
        hate it.

Precious or vile, how dare we seize that offering,
Scatter it, spurn it, in its way to heaven,
Because we know it not ? the sovran lord
Accepts his tribute, myrrh and frankincense
From some, from others penitence and prayer :
Why intercept them from his gracious hand ?
Why dash them down ? why smite the supplicant ?

    Hernando. 'Tis what they do.

    Julian.   Avoid it thou the more.

If time were left me, I could hear well-pleased
How Tarik fought up Calpe's fabled cliff,
While I pursued the friends of Don Roderigo
Across the plain, and drew fresh force from mine.
O ! had some other land, some other cause,
Invited him and me, I then could dwell
On this hard battle with unmixt delight.

    Hernando. Eternal is its glory, if the deed
Be not forgotten till it be surpast :
Much praise by land, by sea much more, he won,

For then a Julian was not at his side,
Nor led the van, nor awed the best before ;
The whole, a mighty whole, was his alone.
There might be seen how far he shone above
All others of the day : old Muza watcht
From his own shore the richly-laden fleet,
Ill-arm'd and scatter'd, and pursued the rear
Beyond those rocks that bear St. Vincent's name,
Cutting the treasure, not the strength, away ;
Valiant, where any prey lies undevour'd
In hostile creek or too confiding isle.
Tarik, with his small barks, but with such love
As never chief from rugged sailor won,
Smote their high masts and swelling rampires down,
And Cadiz wept in fear o'er Trafalgar.
Who that beheld our sails from off the highths,
Like the white birds, nor larger, tempt the gale
In sunshine and in shade, now almost touch
The solitary shore, glance, turn, retire,
Would think these lovely playmates could portend
Such mischief to the world, such blood, such woe ;
Could draw to them from far the peaceful hinds,
Cull the gay flower of cities, and divide
Friends, children, every bond of human life ;
Could dissipate whole families, could sink
Whole states in ruin, at one hour, one blow ?

    Julian. Go, good Hernando ! who *would* think
       these things ?
Say to the valiant Tarik I depart
Forthwith : he knows not from what heaviness

Of soul I linger here ; I could endure
No converse, no compassion, no approach,
Other than thine, whom the same cares improved
Beneath my father's roof, my foster-brother,
To brighter days and happier end, I hope ;
In whose fidelity my own resides
With Tarik and with his compeers and chief.
I cannot share the gladness I excite,
Yet shall our Tarik's generous heart rejoice.

FOURTH ACT: THIRD SCENE.

EGILONA *enters* . HERNANDO *goes.*

Egilona. O fly me not because I am unhappy,
Because I am deserted fly me not ;
It was not so before, and can it be
Ever from Julian ?
Julian.   What would Egilona
That Julian's power with her new lords can do ?
Surely her own must there preponderate.
Egilona. I hold no suit to them.   Restore, restore
Roderigo.
Julian.   He no longer is my prisoner.
Egilona. Escapes he then ?
Julian.   Escapes he, dost thou say ?
O Egilona ! what unworthy passion——
Egilona. Unworthy, when I loved him, was my
          passion ;
The passion that now swells my heart is just.

Julian. What fresh reproaches hath he merited?

Egilona. Deep-rooted hatred shelters no reproach.
But whither is he gone?

Julian.   Far from the walls.

Egilona. And I knew nothing?

Julian.   His offence was known
To thee at least.

Egilona.   Will it be expiated?

Julian. I trust it will.

Egilona.   This withering calm consumes me.
He marries then Covilla! 'twas for this
His people were excited to rebel,
His sceptre was thrown by, his vows were scorn'd,
And I—and I——

Julian.   Cease, Egilona!

Egilona.   Cease?
Sooner shalt thou to live than I to reign.

FIFTH ACT : FIRST SCENE.

Tent of MUZA.

MUZA.   TARIK.   ABDALAZIS.

Muza. To have first landed on these shores appears
Transcendent glory to the applauded Tarik.

Tarik. Glory, but not transcendent, it appears,
What might in any other.

Muza.   Of thyself
All this vain boast?

Tarik.   Not of myself: 'twas Julian.

Against his shield the refluent surges roll'd,
While the sea-breezes threw the arrows wide,
And fainter cheers urged the reluctant steeds.
    Muza. That Julian, of whose treason I have proofs,
That Julian, who rejected my commands
Twice, when our mortal foe besieged the camp,
And forced my princely presence to his tent.
    Tarik. Say rather, who without one exhortation,
One precious drop from true believer's vein,
Marcht, and discomfited our enemies.
I found in him no treachery.   Hernando,
Who, little versed in moody wiles, is gone
To lead him hither, was by him assign'd
My guide, and twice in doubtful fight his arm
Protected me : once on the highths of Calpe,
Once on the plain, when courtly jealousies
Tore from the bravest and the best his due,
And gave the dotard and the coward command :
Then came Roderigo forth : the front of war
Grew darker : him, equal in chivalry,
Julian alone could with success oppose.
    Abdalazis. I doubt their worth who praise their
       enemies.
    Tarik. And theirs doubt I who persecute their
       friends.
    Muza. Thou art in league with him.
    Tarik.   Thou wert, by oaths ;
I am without them ; for his heart is brave.
    Muza. Am I to bear all this ?
    Tarik.   All this and more :

Soon wilt thou see the man whom thou hast wrong'd,
And the keen hatred in thy breast conceal'd
Find its right way, and sting thee to the core.
 Muza. Hath he not foil'd us in the field? not held
Our wisdom to reproach?
 Tarik.   Shall we abandon
All he hath left us in the eyes of men?
Shall we again make him our adversary
Whom we have proved so, long and fatally?
If he subdue for us our enemies,
Shall we raise others, or, for want of them,
Convert him into one against his will?

FIFTH ACT: SECOND SCENE.

HERNANDO *enters.* TARIK *continues.*

Here comes Hernando from that prince himself.
 Muza. Who scorns, himself, to come.
 Hernando.   The queen detains him.
 Abdalazis. How! Egilona?
 Muza.   'Twas my will.
 Tarik.   At last
He must be happy; for delicious calm
Follows the fierce enjoyment of revenge.
 Hernando. That calm was never his, no other will be.
Thou knowest not, and mayst thou never know,
How bitter is the tear that fiery shame
Scourges and tortures from the soldier's eye.
Whichever of these bad reports be true,

He hides it from all hearts to wring his own,
And drags the heavy secret to the grave.
Not victory that o'ershadows him sees he;
No airy and light passion stirs abroad
To ruffle or to soothe him; all are quell'd
Beneath a mightier, sterner stress of mind:
Wakeful he sits, and lonely, and unmoved,
Beyond the arrows, views, or shouts of men;
As oftentimes an eagle, ere the sun
Throws o'er the varying earth his early ray,
Stands solitary, stands immovable
Upon some highest cliff, and rolls his eye,
Clear, constant, unobservant, unabased,
In the cold light above the dews of morn.
He now assumes that quietness of soul
Which never but in danger have I seen
On his staid breast.
  Tarik.   Danger is past; he conquers;
No enemy is left him to subdue.
  Hernando. He sank not, while there was, into him-
   self.
Now plainly see I from his alter'd tone.
He cannot live much longer. Thanks to God!
  Tarik. What! wishest thou thy once kind master
   dead?
Was he not kind to thee, ungrateful slave!
  Hernando. The gentlest, as the bravest, of mankind.
Therefore shall memory dwell more tranquilly
With Julian once at rest, than friendship could,
Knowing him yearn for death with speechless love.

For his own sake I could endure his loss,
Pray for it, and thank God ; yet mourn I must
Him above all, so great, so bountiful,
So blessed once ! bitterly must I mourn.
'Tis not my solace that 'tis his desire ;
Of all who pass us in life's drear descent
We grieve the most for those that wisht to die.
A father to us all, he merited,
Unhappy man ! all a good father's joy
In his own house, where seldom he hath been,
But, ever mindful of its dear delights,
He form'd one family around him ever.
    Tarik. Yes, we have seen and known him.   Let
        his fame
Refresh his friends, but let it stream afar,
Nor in the twilight of home-scenes be lost.
He chose the best, and cherisht them ; he left
To self-reproof the mutinies of vice ;
Avarice, that dwarfs Ambition's tone and mien ;
Envy, sick nursling of the court ; and Pride
That cannot bear his semblance nor himself ;
And Malice, with blear visage half-descried
Amid the shadows of her hiding-place.
    Hernando. What could I not endure, O gallant man,
To hear him spoken of as thou hast spoken !
Oh ! I would almost be a slave to him
Who calls me one.
    Muza.   What ! art thou not ? begone.
    Tarik. Reply not, brave Hernando, but retire.
All can revile, few only can reward.

Behold the meed our mighty chief bestows !
Accept it for thy services, and mine.
More, my bold Spaniard, hath obedience won
Than anger, even in the ranks of war.
   Hernando. The soldier, not the Spaniard, shall
      obey.   *[Goes.*
   Muza (to TARIK). Into our very council bringest
      thou
Children of reprobation and perdition ?
Darkness thy deeds and emptiness thy speech,
Such images thou raisest as buffoons
Carry in merriment on festivals ;
Nor worthiness nor wisdom would display
To public notice their deformities,
Nor cherish them nor fear them ; why shouldst thou ?
   Tarik. I fear not them nor thee.

FIFTH ACT: THIRD SCENE.

EGILONA *enters.*

   Abdalazis.   Advance, O queen.
Now let the turbulence of faction cease.
   Muza. Whate'er thy purpose, speak, and be com-
      posed.
   Egilona. He goes; he is afar ; he follows her ;
He leads her to the altar, to the throne ;
For, calm in vengeance, wise in wickedness,
The traitor hath prevail'd, o'er him, o'er me,
O'er you, the slaves, the dupes, the scorn, of Julian.

What have I heard ! what have I seen !
   Muza.   Proceed.
   Abdalazis. And I swear vengeance on his guilty
      head
Who intercepts from thee the golden rays
Of sovranty, who dares rescind thy rights,
Who steals upon thy rest, and breathes around
Empoison'd damps o'er that serenity
Which leaves the world, and faintly lingers here.
   Muza. Who shuns thee——
   Abdalazis.   Whose desertion
      interdicts
Homage, authority, precedency——
   Muza. Till war shall rescue them——
   Abdalazis.   And love restore.
   Egilona. O generous Abdalazis ! never ! never !
My enemies—Julian alone remains—
The worst in safety, far beyond my reach,
Breathe freely on the summit of their hopes,
Because they never stopt, because they sprang
From crime to crime, and trampled down remorse.
Oh ! if her heart knew tenderness like mine !
Grant vengeance on the guilty ; grant but that,
I ask no more ; my hand, my crown is thine.
Fulfil the justice of offended heaven,
Assert the sacred rights of royalty,
Come not in vain, crush the rebellious crew,
Crush, I implore, the indifferent and supine.
   Muza. Roderigo thus escaped from Julian's tent ?
   Egilona. No, not escaped, escorted, like a king.

The base Covilla first pursued her way
On foot ; but after her the royal car,
Which bore me from San Pablo's to the throne,
Empty indeed, yet ready at her voice,
Roll'd o'er the plain amid the carcases
Of those who fell in battle or in flight :
She, a deceiver still, to whate'er speed
The moment might incite her, often stopt
To mingle prayers with the departing breath,
Improvident ! and those with heavy wounds
Groan'd bitterly beneath her tottering knee.
 Tarik. Now, by the clement and the merciful !
The girl did well. When I breathe out my soul,
Oh ! if compassion give one pang the more,
That pang be mine ; here be it, in this land :
Such women are they in this land alone.
 Egilona. Insulting man !
 Muza.   We shall confound him yet.
Say, and speak quickly, whither went the king ?
Thou knewest where was Julian.
 Abdalazis.   I will tell
Without his answer : yes, my friends ! yes, Tarik,
Now will I speak, nor thou for once reply.
There is, I hear, a poor half-ruined cell
In Xeres, whither few indeed resort,
Green are the walls within, green is the floor
And slippery from disuse ; for christian feet
Avoid it, as half-holy, half-accurst.
Still in its dark recess fanatic Sin
Abases to the ground his tangled hair,

And servile scourges and reluctant groans
Roll o'er the vault uninterruptedly,
Till (such the natural stillness of the place)
The very tear upon the damps below
Drops audible, and the heart's throb replies.
There is the idol maid of christian creed,
And taller images whose history
I know not nor inquired.   A scene of blood,
Of resignation amid mortal pangs,
And other things exceeding all belief.
Hither the aged Opas of Seville
Walkt slowly, and behind him was a man
Barefooted, bruised, dejected, comfortless,
In sackcloth ; the white ashes on his head
Dropt as he smote his breast ; he gather'd up,
Replaced them all, groan'd deeply, lookt to heaven,
And held them like a treasure with claspt hands.

Egilona. O ! was Roderigo so abased ?
Muza.   'Twas he.
Now, Egilona, judge between your friends
And enemies : behold what wretches brought
The king, thy lord, Roderigo, to disgrace.

Egilona. He merited—but not from them—from me
This, and much worse : had I inflicted it,
I had rejoiced—at what I ill endure.

Muza. For thee, for thee alone, we wisht him here,
But other hands release him.

Abdalazis.   With what aim
Will soon appear to those discerning eyes.

Egilona. I pray thee, tell what past until that hour.

Abdalazis. Few words, and indistinct : repentant
    sobs
Fill'd the whole space; the taper in his hand,
Lighting two small dim lamps before the altar,
He gave to Opas ; at the idol's feet
He laid his crown, and wiped his tears away.
The crown reverts not, but the tears return.
    Egilona. Yes, Abdalazis ! soon, abundantly.
If he had only call'd upon my name,
Seeking my pardon ere he lookt to heaven's,
I could have—no ! he thought not once on me !
Never shall he find peace or confidence;
I will rely on fortune and on thee,
Nor fear my future lot : sure, Abdalazis,
A fall so great can never happen twice,
Nor man again be faithless, like Roderigo.
    Abdalazis. Faithless he may be still, never so faith-
    less.
Fainter must be the charms, remote the days,
When memory and dread example die,
When love and terror thrill the heart no more,
And Egilona is herself forgotten.

FIFTH ACT : FOURTH SCENE.

JULIAN *enters.*

Tarik. Turn, and behold him ! who is now con-
    founded ?
Ye who awaited him, where are ye ? speak.
Is some close comet blazing o'er your tents?

Muza ! Abdalazis ! princes ! conquerors !
Summon, interrogate, command, condemn.
   Muza. Justly, Don Julian—but respect for rank
Allays resentment, nor interrogates
Without due form—justly may we accuse
This absence from our councils, from our camp;
This loneliness in which we still remain
Who came invited to redress your wrongs.
Where is the king ?
   Julian.   The people must decide.
   Muza. Imperfectly, I hope, I understand
Those words, unworthy of thy birth and age.
   Julian O chieftain, such have been our Gothic
     laws.
   Muza. Who then amid such turbulence is safe?
   Julian. He who observes them : 'tis no turbulence,
It violates no peace : 'tis surely worth
A voice, a breath of air, thus to create
By their high will the man, form'd after them
In their own image, vested with their power,
To whom they trust their freedom and their lives.
   Muza. They trust ! the people ! God assigns the
     charge,
Kings open but the book of destiny
And read their names; all that remains for them
The mystic hand from time to time reveals.
Worst of idolaters ! idolater
Of that refractory and craving beast
Whose den is in the city, at thy hand
I claim our common enemy, the king.

Julian. Sacred from justice then ! but not from
  malice !

Tarik. Surrender him, my friend. be sure his pains
Will not be soften'd.

Julian.   'Tis beyond my power.

Tarik. To-morrow—if in any distant fort
He lies to-night : send after him.

Julian.   My faith
Is plighted, and he lives—no prisoner.

Egilona. I knew the truth.

Abdalazis (*to* JULIAN). Now, Tarik, hear and
  judge.
Was he not in thy camp? and in disguise?

Tarik. No : I will answer thee.

Muza.   Audacious man !
Had not the Kalif Walid placed thee here,
Chains and a traitor's death should be thy doom.
Speak, Abdalazis ! Egilona, speak.
Were ye not present? was not I myself?
And aided not this Julian his escape?

Julian. 'Tis true.

Tarik.   Away then friendship ! to thy fate
I leave thee : thou hast render'd Muza just,
Me hostile to thee.   Who is safe? a man
Arm'd with such power and with such perfidy !

Julian. Stay, Tarik ! hear me ; for to thee alone
Would I reply.

Tarik.   Thou hast replied already.

                                    [*Goes.*

Muza. We, who were enemies, would not inquire

Too narrowly what reasons urged thy wrath
Against thy sovran lord : beneath his flag
The Christians first assail'd us from these shores,
And we seiz'd gladly the first aid we found
To quell a wealthy and a warlike king.
We never held to thee the vain pretence
That 'twas thy quarrel our brave youth espoused,
Thine, who hast wrought us much disgrace and
    woe
From perils and from losses here we rest
And drink of the fresh fountain at our feet,
Not madly following such illusive streams
As overspread the dizzy wilderness,
And vanish from the thirst they have seduced.
Ours was the enterprise, the land is ours.
What gain we by our toils, if he escape
Whom we came hither solely to subdue?
 Julian. Is there no gain to live in amity?
 Muza. The gain of traffickers and idle men ;
Courage and zeal expire upon such calms.
Further, what amity can Moors expect
When you have joined your forces ?
 Julian.   From the hour
That he was vanquisht, I have laid aside
All power, all arms.
 Muza.   How can we trust thee, once
Deceived, and oftener than this once despised ?
Thou camest hither with no other aim
Than to deprive Roderigo of his crown
For thy own brow.

Egilona.   Julian, base man, 'tis true.
He comes a prince, no warrior, at this hour.
    Muza. His sword, O queen, would not avail him now.
    Abdalazis. Julian, I feel less anger than regret.
No violence of speech, no obloquy,
No accusation shall escape my lips :
Need there is none, nor reason, to avoid
My questions : if thou value truth, reply.
Hath not Roderigo left the town and camp ?
Hath not thy daughter ?
    Egilona.   Past the little brook
Toward the Betis.   From a tower I saw
The fugitives, far on their way ; they went
Over one bridge, each with arm'd men—not half
A league of road between them—and had join'd,
But that the olive-groves along the path
Conceal'd them from each other, not from me :
Beneath me the whole level I survey'd,
And, when my eyes no longer could discern
Which track they took, I knew it from the storks
Rising in clouds above the reedy plain.
    Muza. Deny it, if thou canst.
    Julian.   I order'd it.
    Abdalazis. None could beside.   Lo ! things in such
        a mass
Falling together on observant minds,
Create suspicion and establish proof :
Wanted there fresh—why not employ our arms ?
Why go alone ?
    Muza.   To parley, to conspire,

To reunite the Spaniards, which we saw,
To give up treaties, close up enmities,
And ratify the deed with Moorish blood.

Julian. Gladly would Spain procure your safe return,
Gladly would pay large treasures for the aid
You brought against oppression.

Muza.   Pay she shall
The treasures of her soil, her ports, her youth :
If she resist, if she tumultuously
Call forth her brigands and we lose a man,
Dreadful shall be our justice ; war shall rage
Through every city, hamlet, house, and field,
And, universal o'er the gasping land,
Depopulation.

Julian.   They shall rue the day
Who dare these things.

Muza.   Let order then prevail.
In vain thou sendest far away thy child,
Thy counsellor the metropolitan,
And Sisabert : prudence is mine no less.
Divide with us our conquests, but the king
Must be deliver'd up.

Julian.   Never by me.

Muza. False then were thy reproaches, false thy grief.

Julian. O Egilona ! were thine also feign'd ?

Abdalazis. Say, lovely queen, neglectful of thy charms
Turn'd he his eyes toward the young Covilla ?

Did he pursue her to the mad excess
Of breaking off her vows to Sisabert,
And marrying her, against the Christian law?
　Muza. Did he prefer her so?
　Abdalazis. 　　　　　　　　Could he prefer
To Egilona——
　Egilona. 　　　　Her! the child Covilla?
Eternal hider of a foolish face,
Incapable of anything but shame,
To me? old man! to me? O Abdalazis!
No: he but follow'd with slow pace my hate.
And cannot pride check these unseemly tears. [*Goes.*
　Muza. The most offended, an offended woman,
A wife, a queen, is silent on the deed.
　Abdalazis. Thou disingenuous and ignoble man,
Spreading these rumours! sending into exile
All those their blighting influence injured most:
And whom? thy daughter and adopted son,
The chieftains of thy laws and of thy faith.
Call any witnesses, proclaim the truth,
And set at last thy heart, thy fame, at rest.
　Julian. Not, if I purposed or desired to live,
My own dishonour would I e'er proclaim
Amid vindictive and reviling foes.
　Muza. Calling us foes, avows he not his guilt?
Condemns he not the action we condemn,
Owning it his, and owning it dishonour?
'Tis well my cares prest forward, and struck home.
　Julian. Why smilest thou? I never saw that smile
But it portended an atrocious deed.

Muza. After our manifold and stern assaults,
With every tower and battlement destroy'd,
The walls of Ceuta still were strong enough——
   Julian. For what? who boasted now her brave
     defence,
Or who forbad your entrance after peace?
   Muza. None: for who could? their engines now
     arose
To throw thy sons into the arms of death.
For this erect they their proud crests again.
Mark him at last turn pale before a Moor.
   Julian. Imprudent have they been, their youth shall
     plead.
   Abdalazis. O father! could they not have been
     detain'd?
   Muza. Son, thou art safe, and wert not while they
     lived.
   Abdalazis. I fear'd them not.
   Muza.   And therefore wert not safe:
Under their star the blooming Egilona
Would watch for thee the nuptial lamp in vain.
   Julian. Never, oh never, hast thou workt a wile
So barren of all good! Speak out at once,
What hopest thou by striking this alarm?
It shocks my reason, not my fears or fondness.
   Muza. Be happy then as ignorance can be;
Soon wilt thou hear it shouted from our ranks.
Those who once hurl'd defiance o'er our heads,
Scorning our arms, and scoffing at our faith,
The nightly wolf hath visited, unscared,

And loathed them as her prey ; for famine first,
Achieving in few days the boast of years,
Sank their young eyes and open'd us the gates :
Ceuta, her port, her citadel, is ours.

    Julian. Blest boys ! inhuman as thou art, what
        guilt
Was theirs ?

    Muza.   Their father's.

    Julian.   O support me, Heaven !
Against this blow ! all others I have borne.
Ermenegild ! thou mightest, sure, have lived !
A father's name awoke no dread of thee !
Only thy mother's early bloom was thine !
There dwelt on Julian's brow—thine was serene—
The brighten'd clouds of elevated souls,
Fear'd by the most below : those who lookt up
Saw at their season in clear signs advance
Rapturous valour, calm solicitude,
All that impatient youth would press from age,
Or sparing age sigh and detract from youth :
Hence was his fall ! my hope ! myself ! my Julian !
Alas ! I boasted—but I thought on him,
Inheritor of all—all what ? my wrongs—
Follower of me—and whither ? to the grave—
Ah no : it should have been so years far hence !
Him at this moment I could pity most,
But I most prided in him ; now I know
I loved a name, I doated on a shade.
Sons ! I approach the mansions of the just,
And my arms clasp you in the same embrace,

Where none shall sever you—and do I weep!
And do they triumph o'er my tenderness!
I had forgotten my inveterate foes
Everywhere nigh me, I had half forgotten
Your very murderers, while I thought on you:
For, O my children, ye fill all the space
My soul would wander o'er—O bounteous heaven!
There is a presence, if the well-beloved
Be torn from us by human violence,
More intimate, pervading, and complete,
Than when they lived and spoke like other men;
And their pale images are our support
When reason sinks, or threatens to desert us.
I weep no more—pity and exultation
Sway and console me : are they—no!—both dead?
 Muza. Ay, and unsepulchred.
 Julian.   Nor wept nor seen
By any kindred and far-following eye?
 Muza. Their mother saw them, if not dead, expire.
 Julian. O cruelty—to them indeed the least!
My children, ye are happy—ye have lived
Of heart unconquer'd, honour unimpair'd,
And died, true Spaniards, loyal to the last.
 Muza. Away with him.
 Julian.   Slaves! not before I lift
My voice to heaven and man : though enemies
Surround me, and none else, yet other men
And other times shall hear : the agony
Of an opprest and of a bursting heart
No violence can silence; at its voice

The trumpet is o'erpower'd, and glory mute,
And peace and war hide all their charms alike.
Surely the guests and ministers of heaven
Scatter it forth through all the elements,
So suddenly, so widely, it extends,
So fearfully men breathe it, shuddering
To ask or fancy how it first arose.
    Muza. Yes, they shall shudder: but will that, henceforth,
Molest my privacy, or shake my power?
    Julian. Guilt hath pavilions, but no privacy.
The very engine of his hatred checks
The torturer in his transport of revenge,
Which, while it swells his bosom, shakes his power,
And raises friends to his worst enemy.
    Muza. Where now are thine? will they not curse the
That gave thee birth, and hiss thy funeral !   [day
Thou hast left none who could have pitied thee.
    Julian. Many, nor those alone of tenderer mould,
For me will weep; many, alas, through me !
Already I behold my funeral ;
The turbid cities wave and swell with it,
And wrongs are lost in that day's pageantry :
Opprest and desolate, the countryman
Receives it like a gift ; he hastens home,
Shows where the hoof of Moorish horse laid waste
His narrow croft and winter garden-plot,
Sweetens with fallen pride his children's lore,
And points their hatred, but applauds their tears.
Justice, who came not up to us through life,

Loves to survey our likeness on our tombs,
When rivalry, malevolence, and wrath,
And every passion that once storm'd around,
Is calm alike without them as within.
Our very chains make the whole world our own,
Bind those to us who else had past us by,
Those at whose call brought down to us, the light
Of future ages lives upon our name.
    Muza. I may accelerate that meteor's fall,
And quench that idle ineffectual light
Than hout the knowledge of thy distant world.
And *Julian.* My world and thine are not that distant one.
Was age less wise, less merciful, than grief,
To keep this secret from thee, poor old man?
    Thou canst not lessen, canst not aggravate
My sufferings, canst not shorten or extend
Half a sword's length between my God and me.
I thank thee for that better thought than fame,
Which none however, who deserve, despise,
Nor lose from view till all things else are lost.
    Abdalazis. Julian, respect his age, regard his power.
Many who fear'd not death, have dragg'd along
A piteous life in darkness and in chains.
Never was man so full of wretchedness
But something may be suffered after all,
Perhaps in what clings round his breast and helps
To keep the ruin up, which he amid
His agony and frenzy overlooks,
But droops upon at last, and clasps, and dies.
    Julian. Although a Muza send far underground,

Into the quarry whence the palace rose,
His mangled prey, climes alien and remote
Mark and record the pang.   While overhead
Perhaps he passes on his favourite steed,
Less heedful of the misery he inflicts
Than of the expiring sparkle from a stone,
Yet we, alive or dead, have fellow-men
If ever we have served them, who collect
From prisons and from dungeons our remains,
And bear them in their bosom to their sons.
Man's only relics are his benefits ;
These, be there ages, be there worlds, between,
Retain him in communion with his kind :
Hence is our solace, our security,
Our sustenance, till heavenly truth descends,
Covering with brightness and beatitude
The frail foundations of these humbler hopes,
And, like an angel guiding us, at once
Leaves the loose chain and iron gate behind.
    Muza. Take thou my justice first, then hope for
        theirs.
I, who can bend the living to my will,
Fear not the dead, and court not the unborn :
Their arm will never reach me, nor shall thine.
    Abdalazis. Pity, release him, pardon him, my father !
Forget how much thou hatest perfidy,
Think of him, once so potent, still so brave,
So calm, so self-dependent in distress,
I marvel at him : hardly dare I blame
When I behold him fallen from so high,

And so exalted after such a fall.
Mighty must that man be, who can forgive
A man so mighty; seize the hour to rise,
Another never comes: O say, my father !
Say, " Julian, be my enemy no more."
He fills me with a greater awe than e'er
The field of battle, with himself the first,
When every flag that waved along our host
Droopt down the staff, as if the very winds
Hung in suspense before him.   Bid him go
And peace be with him, or let me depart.
Lo ! like a god, sole and inscrutable,
He stands above our pity.
   Julian.   For that wish—
Vain as it is, 'tis virtuous—O, for that,
However wrong thy censure and thy praise,
Kind Abdalazis ! mayst thou never feel
The rancour that consumes thy father's breast,
Nor want the pity thou hast sought for mine !
   Muza. Now hast thou seal'd thy doom.
   Julian.   And thou thy crimes.
   Abdalazis. O father ! heed him not: those evil
      words
Leave neither blight nor blemish: let him go.
   Muza. A boy, a very boy art thou indeed !
One who in early day would sally out
To chase the lion, and would call it sport,
But, when more wary steps had closed him round,
Slink from the circle, drop the toils, and blanch
Like a lithe plant from under snow in spring.

Abdalazis. He who ne'er shrank from danger might
    shrink now,
And ignominy would not follow here.
    Muza. Peace, Abdalazis! How is this? he bears
Nothing that warrants him invulnerable :
Shall I then shrink to smite him? shall my fears
Be greatest at the blow that ends them all?
Fears? no! 'tis justice, fair, immutable,
Whose measured step at times advancing nigh
Appalls the majesty of kings themselves.
O were he dead! though then revenge were o'er.

FIFTH ACT: FIFTH SCENE.

Officer. Thy wife, Count Julian!
Julian   Speak!
Officer.   Is dead.
Julian.   Adieu
Earth! and the humblest of all earthly hopes,
To hear of comfort, though to find it vain.
Thou murderer of the helpless! shame of man!
Shame of thy own base nature! 'tis an act
He who could perpetrate could not avow,
Stain'd, as he boasts to be, with innocent blood,
Deaf to reproach and blind to retribution.
    Officer. Julian! be just; 'twill make thee less
    unhappy.
Grief was her end : she held her younger boy
And wept upon his cheek; his naked breast
By recent death now hardening and inert,

Slipt from her knee ; again with frantic grasp
She caught it, and it weigh'd her to the ground :
There lay the dead.

  Julian.   She?

  Officer.   And the youth her son.

  Julian. Receive them to thy peace, eternal God !
O soother of my hours, while I beheld
The light of day, and thine ! adieu, adieu !
And, my Covilla ! dost thou yet survive?
Yes, my lost child, thou livest yet—in shame !
O agony, past utterance ! past thought !
That throwest death, as some light idle thing,
With all its terrors, into dust and air,
I will endure thee ; I, whom heaven ordain'd
Thus to have serv'd beneath my enemies,
Their conqueror, thus to have revisited
My native land with vengeance and with woe.
Henceforward shall she recognise her sons,
Impatient of oppression or disgrace,
And rescue them, or perish ; let her hold
This compact, written with her blood and mine.
Now follow me : but tremble : years shall roll
And wars rage on, and Spain at last be free.

Miscellaneous Poems.

Collection of 1846.

SELECTIONS.

---◆◆◆---

I.

THE touch of Love dispels the gloom
Of life, and animates the tomb;
But never let it idly flare
On gazers in the open air,
Nor turn it quite away from one
To whom it serves for moon and sun,
And who alike in night or day
Without it could not find his way.

II.

She I love (alas in vain !)
 Floats before my slumbering eyes:
When she comes she lulls my pain,
 When she goes what pangs arise !
Thou whom love, whom memory flies,
 Gentle Sleep ! prolong thy reign !
If even thus she soothe my sighs,
 Never let me wake again !

III.

Thou hast not rais'd, Ianthe, such desire
   In any breast as thou hast rais'd in mine.
No wandering meteor now, no marshy fire,
   Leads on my steps, but lofty, but divine :
And, if thou chillest me, as chill thou dost
   When I approach too near, too boldly gaze,
So chills the blushing morn, so chills the host
   Of vernal stars, with light more chaste than day's.

IV.

PLEASURE ! why thus desert the heart
    In its spring-tide?
I could have seen her, I could part,
    And but have sigh'd !

O'er every youthful charm to stray,
    To gaze, to touch—
Pleasure ! why take so much away,
    Or give so much?

V.

My hopes retire ; my wishes as before
Struggle to find their resting-place in vain :
The ebbing sun thus beats against the shore ;
The shore repels it ; it returns again.

VI.

O THOU whose happy pencil strays
Where I am call'd, nor dare to gaze,
  But lower my eye and check my tongue;
O, if thou valuest peaceful days,
Pursue the ringlet's sunny maze,
  And dwell not on those lips too long.

What mists athwart my temples fly,
Now, touch by touch, thy fingers tie
  With torturing care her graceful zone !
For all that sparkles from her eye
I could not look while thou art by,
  Nor could I cease were I alone.

VII.

ALL tender thoughts that e'er possest
The human brain or human breast,
   Centre in mine for thee—
Excepting one—and that must thou
Contribute : come, confer it now :
   Grateful I fain would be.

VIII.

Past ruin'd Ilion Helen lives,
    Alcestis rises from the shades;
Verse calls them forth; 'tis verse that gives
    Immortal youth to mortal maids.

Soon shall Oblivion's deepening veil
    Hide all the peopled hills you see,
The gay, the proud, while lovers hail
    These many summers you and me.

IX.

ONE year ago my path was green,
My footstep light, my brow serene;
Alas! and could it have been so
      One year ago?
There is a love that is to last
When the hot days of youth are past:
Such love did a sweet maid bestow
      One year ago.
I took a leaflet from her braid
And gave it to another maid.
Love! broken should have been thy bow
      One year ago.

X.

I CANNOT tell, not I, why she
Awhile so gracious, now should be
So grave : I cannot tell you why
The violet hangs its head awry.
It shall be cull'd, it shall be worn,
In spite of every sign of scorn,
Dark look, and overhanging thorn.

XI.

FROM you, Ianthe, little troubles pass
　Like little ripples down a sunny river;
Your pleasures spring like daisies in the grass,
　Cut down, and up again as blithe as ever.

XII.

IANTHE ! you are call'd to cross the sea !
        A path forbidden *me !*
Remember, while the Sun his blessing sheds
        Upon the mountain-heads,
How often we have watcht him laying down
        His brow, and dropt our own
Against each other's, and how faint and short
        And sliding the support !
What will succeed it now ?   Mine is unblest,
        Ianthe ! nor will rest
But on the very thought that swells with pain.
        O bid me hope again !
O give me back what Earth, what (without you)
        Not Heaven itself can do,
One of the golden days that we have past ;
        And let it be my last !
Or else the gift would be, however sweet,
Fragile and incomplete.

XIII.

If mutable is she I love,
  If rising doubts demand their place,
I would adjure them not to move
  Beyond her fascinating face.

Let it be question'd, while there flashes
  A liquid light of fleeting blue,
Whether it leaves the eyes or lashes,
  Plays on the surface or peeps through.

With every word let there appear
  So modest yet so sweet a smile,
That he who hopes must gently fear,
  Who fears may fondly hope the while.

XIV.

ACCORDING to eternal laws
('Tis useless to inquire the cause)
The gates of fame and of the grave
Stand under the same architrave,
So I would rather some time yet
Play on with you, my little pet !

XV.

You tell me I must come again
  Now buds and blooms appear :
Ah ! never fell one word in vain
  Of yours on mortal ear.
You say the birds are busy now
  In hedgerow, brake, and grove,
And slant their eyes to find the bough
  That best conceals their love :
How many warble from the spray !
  How many on the wing !
" Yet, yet," say you, " one voice away
  I miss the sound of spring."
How little could that voice express,
  Beloved, when we met !
But other sounds hath tenderness,
  Which neither shall forget.

XVI.

YE walls ! sole witnesses of happy sighs,
  Say not, blest walls, one word.
Remember, but keep safe from ears and eyes
  All you have seen and heard.

XVII.

ALONG this coast I led the vacant Hours
   To the lone sunshine on the uneven strand,
And nipt the stubborn grass and juicier flowers
   With one unconscious inobservant hand,
While crept the other by degrees more near
   Until it rose the cherisht form around,
And prest it closer, only that the ear
   Might lean, and deeper drink some half-heard
     sound.

XVIII.

PURSUITS! alas, I now have none,
  But idling where were once pursuits,
Often, all morning quite alone,
  I sit upon those twisted roots
Which rise above the grass, and shield
  Our harebell, when the churlish year
Catches her coming first afield,
  And she looks pale tho' spring is near;
I chase the violets, that would hide
  Their little prudish heads away,
And argue with the rills, that chide
  When we discover them at play.

XIX.

TWENTY years hence my eyes may grow
If not quite dim, yet rather so,
Still yours from others they shall know
               Twenty years hence.
Twenty years hence tho' it may hap
That I be call'd to take a nap
In a cool cell where thunder-clap
               Was never heard.

There breathe but o'er my arch of grass
A not too sadly sigh'd *Alas,*
And I shall catch, ere you can pass,
               That winged word.

XX.

REMAIN, ah not in youth alone,
　Tho' youth, where you are, long will stay,
But when my summer days are gone,
　And my autumnal haste away.
" *Can I be always by your side ?* "
　No ; but the hours you can, you must,
Nor rise at Death's approaching stride,
　Nor go when dust is gone to dust.

XXI.

HERE, ever since you went abroad,
  If there be change, no change I see,
I only walk our wonted road,
  The road is only walkt by me.

Yes; I forgot ; a change there is ;
  Was it of *that* you bade me tell ?
I catch at times, at times I miss
  The sight, the tone, I know so well.

Only two months since you stood here !
  Two shortest months ! then tell me why
Voices are harsher than they were,
  And tears are longer ere they dry.

XXII.

As round the parting ray the busy motes
  In eddying circles play'd,
Some little bird threw dull and broken notes
  Amid an elder's shade.

My soul was tranquil as the scene around,
  Ianthe at my side ;
Both leaning silent on the turfy mound,
  Lowly and soft and wide.

I had not lookt, that evening, for the part
  One hand could disengage,
To make her arms cling round me, with a start
  My bosom must assuage :

Silence and soft inaction please as much
  Sometimes the stiller breast,
Which passion now has thrill'd with milder touch
  And love in peace possest.

" Hark ! hear you not the nightingale ? " I said,
 To strike her with surprise.
" The nightingale ? " she cried, and raised her head,
 And beam'd with brighter eyes.

" Before you said 'twas he that piped above,
 At every thrilling swell
He pleas'd me more and more ; he sang of love
 So plaintively, so well."

Where are ye, happy days, when every bird
 Pour'd love in every strain ?
Ye days, when true was every idle word,
 Return, return again !

XXIII.

MILD is the parting year, and sweet
   The odour of the falling spray ;
Life passes on more rudely fleet,
   And balmless is its closing day.
I wait its close, I court its gloom,
   But mourn that never must there fall
Or on my breast or on my tomb
   The tear that would have sooth'd it all.

XXIV.

THANK Heaven, Ianthe, once again
 Our hands and ardent lips shall meet,
And Pleasure, to assert his reign,
 Scatter ten thousand kisses sweet :
Then cease repeating while you mourn,
" I wonder when he will return."

Ah wherefore should you so admire
 The flowing words that fill my song,
Why call them artless, yet require
 " Some promise from that tuneful tongue ? "
I doubt if heaven itself could part
A tuneful tongue and tender heart.

XXV.

THERE are some wishes that may start
Nor cloud the brow nor sting the heart.
Gladly then would I see how smiled
One who now fondles with her child ;
How smiled she but six years ago,
Herself a child, or nearly so.
Yes, let me bring before my sight
The silken tresses chain'd up tight,
The tiny fingers tipt with red
By tossing up the strawberry-bed ;
Half-open lips, long violet eyes,
A little rounder with surprise,
And then (her chin against the knee)
" Mamma ! who can that stranger be?
How grave the smile he smiles on me ! "

XXVI.

FROM yonder wood mark blue-eyed Eve proceed :
First thro' the deep and warm and secret glens,
Thro' the pale-glimmering privet-scented lane,
And thro' those alders by the river-side :
Now the soft dust impedes her, which the sheep
Have hollow'd out beneath their hawthorn shade.
But ah ! look yonder ! see a misty tide
Rise up the hill, lay low the frowning grove,
Enwrap the gay white mansion, sap its sides
Until they sink and melt away like chalk ;
Now it comes down against our village-tower,
Covers its base, floats o'er its arches, tears
The clinging ivy from the battlements,
Mingles in broad embrace the obdurate stone,
(All one vast ocean), and goes swelling on
In slow and silent, dim and deepening waves.

XXVII.

In Clementina's artless mien
    Lucilla asks me what I see,
And are the roses of sixteen
        Enough for me?

Lucilla asks, if that be all,
    Have I not cull'd as sweet before:
Ah yes, Lucilla! and their fall
        I still deplore.

I now behold another scene,
    Where Pleasure beams with heaven's
        own light,
More pure, more constant, more serene,
        And not less bright:

Faith, on whose breast the Loves repose,
    Whose chain of flowers no force can
        sever,
And Modesty who, when she goes,
        Is gone for ever.

XXVIII.

Mother, I cannot mind my wheel ;
My fingers ache, my lips are dry :
Oh ! if you felt the pain I feel !
But oh, who ever felt as I?
No longer could I doubt him true—
All other men may use deceit ;
He always said my eyes were blue,
And often swore my lips were sweet.

XXIX.

AH what avails the sceptred race,
 Ah what the form divine !
What every virtue, every grace !
 Rose Aylmer, all were thine.
Rose Aylmer, whom these wakeful eyes
 May weep, but never see,
A night of memories and of sighs
 I consecrate to thee.

XXX.

I COME to visit thee again,
My little flowerless cyclamen !
To touch the hands, almost to press,
That cheer'd thee in thy loneliness.
What could those lovely sisters find,
Of thee in form, of me in mind,
What is there in us rich or rare,
To make us worth a moment's care ?
Unworthy to be so carest,
We are but wither'd leaves at best.

XXXI.

"You must give back," her mother said
To a poor sobbing little maid,
"All the young man has given you,
Hard as it now may seem to do."
  "'Tis done already, mother dear!"
Said the sweet girl, "So, never fear."
  Mother. Are you quite certain?   Come, recount
(There was not much) the whole amount.
  Girl. The locket: the kid gloves.
  Mother.   Go on.
  Girl. Of the kid gloves I found but one.
  Mother. Never mind that.   What else?   Proceed.
You gave back all his trash?
  Girl.   Indeed.
  Mother. And was there nothing you would save?
  Girl. Everything I could give I gave.
  Mother. To the last tittle?
  Girl.   Even to that.
  Mother. Freely?
  Girl. My heart went *pit-a-pat*
At giving up—ah me! ah me!
I cry so I can hardly see—
All the fond looks and words that past,
And all the kisses, to the last.

XXXII.

THE maid I love ne'er thought of me
Amid the scenes of gaiety;
But when her heart or mine sank low,
Ah then it was no longer so.
From the slant palm she rais'd her head,
And kist the cheek whence youth had fled.
Angels! some future day for this,
Give her as sweet and pure a kiss.

XXXIII.

WHY, why repine, my pensive friend,
    At pleasures slipt away?
Some the stern Fates will never lend,
    And all refuse to stay.

I see the rainbow in the sky,
    The dew upon the grass,
I see them, and I ask not why
    They glimmer or they pass.

With folded arms I linger not
    To call them back; 'twere vain;
In this, or in some other spot,
    I know they'll shine again.

XXXIV.

The burden of an ancient rhyme
Is, " By the forelock seize on Time."
Time in some corner heard it said ;
Pricking his ears, away he fled ;
And, seeing me upon the road,
A hearty curse on me bestow'd.
" What if I do the same by thee?
How wouldst thou like it ? " thunder'd he,
And, without answer thereupon,
Seizing *my* forelock—it was gone.

XXXV.

WILL mortals never know each other's station
Without the herald ?   O abomination !
Milton, even Milton, rankt with living men !
Over the highest Alps of mind he marches,
And far below him spring the baseless arches
Of Iris, colouring dimly lake and fen.

XXXVI.

TELL me, perverse young year!
Why is the morn so drear?
   Is there no flower to twine?
Away, thou churl, away
'Tis Rose's natal day,
   Reserve thy frown for mine.

XXXVII.

A SEA-SHELL SPEAKS.

Of late among the rocks I lay,
But just behind the fretful spray,
When suddenly a step drew near,
And a man's voice, distinct and clear,
Convey'd this solace—
                                    " Come with me,
Thou little outcast of the sea !
Our destiny, poor shell, is one ;
We both may shine, but shine alone :
Both are deprived of all we had
In earlier days to make us glad,
Or ask us why we should be sad :
Which (you may doubt it as you will)
To manly hearts is dearer still."
I felt, ere half these words were o'er,
A few salt drops on me once more.

/

XXXVIII.

OFTEN I have heard it said
That her lips are ruby-red.
Little heed I what they say,
I have seen as red as they.
Ere she smiled on other men,
Real rubies were they then.

When she kist me once in play,
Rubies were less bright than they,
And less bright were those which shone
In the palace of the Sun.
Will they be as bright again?
Not if kist by other men.

XXXIX.

In spring and summer winds may blow,
　And rains fall after, hard and fast;
The tender leaves, if beaten low,
　Shine but the more for shower and blast.

But when their fated hour arrives,
　When reapers long have left the field,
When maidens rifle turn'd-up hives,
　And their last juice fresh apples yield,

A leaf perhaps may still remain
　Upon some solitary tree,
Spite of the wind and of the rain—
　A thing you heed not if you see—

At last it falls.　Who cares? not one:
　And yet no power on earth can ever
Replace the fallen leaf upon
　Its spray, so easy to dissever.

If such be love I dare not say,
　Friendship is such, too well I know;
I have enjoy'd my summer day;
　'Tis past; my leaf now lies below.

XL.

VERY true, the linnets sing
Sweetest in the leaves of spring :
You have found in all these leaves
That which changes and deceives,
And, to pine by sun or star,
Left them, false ones as they are.
But there be who walk beside
Autumn's, till they all have died,
And who lend a patient ear
To low notes from branches sere.

XLI.

FAREWELL TO ITALY.

I LEAVE thee, beauteous Italy ! no more
From the high terraces, at eventide,
To look supine into thy depths of sky,
Thy golden moon between the cliff and me,
Or thy dark spires of fretted cypresses
Bordering the channel of the milky-way.
Fiesole and Valdarno must be dreams
Hereafter, and my own lost Affrico
Murmur to me but in the poet's song.
I did believe (what have I not believed?)
Weary with age, but unopprest by pain,
To close in thy soft clime my quiet day
And rest my bones in the Mimosa's shade.
Hope ! Hope ! few ever cherisht thee so little ;
Few are the heads thou hast so rarely raised ;
But thou didst promise this, and all was well.
For we are fond of thinking where to lie
When every pulse hath ceast, when the lone heart

Can lift no aspiration—reasoning
As if the sight were unimpaired by death,
Were unobstructed by the coffin-lid,
And the sun cheered corruption!   Over all
The smiles of Nature shed a potent charm,
And light us to our chamber at the grave.

XLII.

VARIOUS the roads of life ; in one
All terminate, one lonely way.
We go ; and " Is he gone? "
Is all our best friends say.

XLIII.

RIGHTLY you say you do not know
How much, my little maid, you owe
    My guardian care. The veriest dunce
Beats me at reckoning. Pray, permit
My modesty to limit it,
    Nor urge me to take all at once.
You are so young, I dare not say
I might demand from you each day
    Of a long life a lawful kiss.
I, so much older, won't repine
If you pay *me* one, each of mine,
    But be exact ; begin with this.

XLIV.

Yes ; I write verses now and then,
But blunt and flaccid is my pen,
No longer talkt of by young men
        As rather clever :

In the last quarter are my eyes,
You see it by their form and size ;
Is it not time then to be wise?
        Or now or never.

Fairest that ever sprang from Eve !
While Time allows the short reprieve,
Just look at me ! would you believe
        'Twas once a lover ?

I cannot clear the five-bar gate,
But, trying first its timber's state,
Climb stiffly up, take breath, and wait
        To trundle over.

Thro' gallopade I cannot swing
The entangling blooms of Beauty's spring :
I cannot say the tender thing,
    Be't true or false,

And am beginning to opine
Those girls are only half-divine
Whose waists yon wicked boys entwine
    In giddy waltz.

I fear that arm above that shoulder,
I wish them wiser, graver, older,
Sedater, and no harm if colder
    And panting less.

Ah ! people were not half so wild
In former days, when, starchly mild,
Upon her high-heel'd Essex smiled
    The brave Queen Bess.

XLV.

TO E. F.

No doubt thy little bosom beats
   When sounds a wedding bell,
No doubt it pants to taste the sweets
   That song and stories tell.

Awhile in shade content to lie,
   Prolong life's morning dream,
While others rise at the first fly
   That glitters on the stream.

XLVI.

Summer has doft his latest green,
  And Autumn ranged the barley-mows.
So long away then have you been?
  And are you coming back to close
  The year? it sadly wants repose.

XLVII.

WHERE three huge dogs are ramping yonder
  Before that villa with its tower,
No braver boys, no father fonder,
  Ever prolong'd the moonlight hour.

Often, to watch their sports unseen,
  Along the broad stone bench he lies,
The oleander-stems between
  And citron-boughs to shade his eyes.

The clouds now whiten far away,
  And villas glimmer thick below,
And windows catch the quivering ray,
  Obscure one minute's space ago.

Orchards and vine-knolls maple-propt
  Rise radiant round : the meads are dim,
As if the milky-way had dropt
  And fill'd Valdarno to the brim.

Unseen beneath us, on the right,
   The abbey with unfinisht front
Of checker'd marble, black and white,
   And on the left the Doccia's font.

Eastward, two ruin'd castles rise
   Beyond Maiano's mossy mill,
Winter and Time their enemies,
   Without their warder, stately still.

The heaps around them there will grow
   Higher, as years sweep by, and higher,
Till every battlement laid low
   Is seized and trampled by the briar.

That line so lucid is the weir
   Of Rovezzano : but behold
The graceful tower of Giotto there,
   And Duomo's cross of freshen'd gold.

We cannot tell, so far away,
   Whether the city's tongue be mute,
We only hear some lover play
   (If sighs be play) the sighing flute.

XLVIII.

THE leaves are falling ; so am I ;
The few late flowers have moisture in the eye ;
    So have I too.
Scarcely on any bough is heard
Joyous, or even unjoyous, bird
    The whole wood through.
Winter may come : he brings but nigher
His circle (yearly narrowing) to the fire
    Where old friends meet :
Let him ; now heaven is overcast,
And spring and summer both are past,
    And all things sweet.

XLIX.

THE place where soon I think to lie,
In its old creviced nook hard-by
    Rears many a weed :
If parties bring you there, will you
Drop slily in a grain or two
    Of wall-flower seed?

I shall not see it, and (too sure !)
I shall not ever hear that your
    Light step was there;
But the rich odour some fine day
Will, what I cannot do, repay
    That little care.

L.

ON RECEIVING A MONTHLY ROSE.

PÆSTUM ! thy roses long ago,
    All roses far above,
Twice in the year were call'd to blow
    And braid the locks of Love.

He saw the city sink in dust,
    Its roses' roots decay'd,
And cried in sorrow, " Find I must
    Another for my braid."

First Cyprus, then the Syrian shore,
    To Pharpar's lucid rill,
Did those two large dark eyes explore,
    But wanted something still.

Damascus fill'd his heart with joy,
    So sweet her roses were !
He cull'd them ; but the wayward boy
    Thought them ill worth his care.

" I want them every month," he cried,
    " I want them every hour :
Perennial rose, and none beside,
    Henceforth shall be my flower."

LI.

FATE! I have askt few things of thee,
  And fewer have to ask.
Shortly, thou knowest, I shall be
  No more: then con thy task.

If one be left on earth so late
  Whose love is like the past,
Tell her in whispers, gentle Fate!
  Not even love must last.

Tell her I leave the noisy feast
  Of life, a little tired,
Amid its pleasures few possest
  And many undesired.

Tell her with steady pace to come
  And, where my laurels lie,
To throw the freshest on the tomb,
  When it has caught her sigh.

Tell her to stand some steps apart
  From others on that day,
And check the tear (if tear should start)
  Too precious for dull clay.

LII.

LADY TO LADY.

TELL me, proud though lovely maiden!
He who heaves from heart o'erladen
Verse on verse for only you,
What is it he hopes to do?

REPLY.

WHAT he hopes is but to please.
If I give his hand a squeeze,
Silent, at the closing strain,
Tell me, does it write in vain?

LIII.

FLOWERS SENT IN BAY-LEAVES.

I LEAVE for you to disunite
    Frail flowers and lasting bays:
One, let me hope, you'll wear to-night,
    The other all your days.

LIV.

SIGHS must be grown less plentiful,
Or else my senses are more dull.
Where are they all ?   These many years
Only mine own have reacht my ears.

LV.

TIME past I thought it worth my while
To hunt all day to catch a smile :
Now ladies do not smile, but laugh,
I like it not so much by half ;
And yet perhaps it might be shown
A laugh is but a smile full-blown.

LVI.

TO ROBERT BROWNING.

THERE is delight in singing, tho' none hear
Beside the singer; and there is delight
In praising, tho' the praiser sit alone
And see the prais'd far off him, far above.
Shakespeare is not our poet, but the world's,
Therefore on him no speech! and brief for thee,
Browning! Since Chaucer was alive and hale,
No man hath walkt along our roads with step
So active, so inquiring eye, or tongue
So varied in discourse. But warmer climes
Give brighter plumage, stronger wing: the breeze
Of Alpine highths thou playest with, borne on
Beyond Sorrento and Amalfi, where
The Siren waits thee, singing song for song.

LVII.

TO THE SISTER OF ELIA.

COMFORT thee, O thou mourner, yet awhile !
  Again shall Elia's smile
Refresh thy heart, where heart can ache no more.
  What is it we deplore ?

He leaves behind him, freed from griefs and years,
  Far worthier things than tears.
The love of friends without a single foe :
  Unequalled lot below !

His gentle soul, his genius, these are thine ;
  For these dost thou repine ?
He may have left the lowly walks of men ;
  Left them he has ; what then ?

Are not his footsteps followed by the eyes
　　　Of all the good and wise?
Tho' the warm day is over, yet they seek
　　　Upon the lofty peak

Of his pure mind the roseate light that glows
　　　O'er death's perennial snows.
Behold him! from the region of the blest
　　　He speaks: he bids thee rest.

LVIII.

DARLING shell, where hast thou been,
West or East? or heard or seen?
From what pastimes art thou come?
Can we make amends at home?

Whether thou hast tuned the dance
    To the maids of ocean
Know I not; but Ignorance
    Never hurts Devotion.

This I know, Ianthe's shell,
I must ever love thee well,
Tho' too little to resound
While the Nereids dance around;

For, of all the shells that are,
    Thou art sure the brightest;
Thou, Ianthe's infant care,
    Most these eyes delightest.

To thy early aid she owes
Teeth like budding snowdrop rows :
And what other shell can say
On her bosom once it lay?

That which into Cyprus bore
  Venus from her native sea,
(Pride of shells !) was never more
  Dear to her than thou to me.

LIX.

BELOVED the last ! beloved the most !
  With willing arms and brow benign
Receive a bosom tempest-tost,
  And bid it ever beat to thine.

The Nereid maids, in days of yore,
  Saw the lost pilot loose the helm,
Saw the wreck blacken all the shore,
  And every wave some head o'erwhelm.

Afar the youngest of the train
  Beheld (but fear'd and aided not)
A minstrel from the billowy main
  Borne breathless near her coral grot.

Then terror fled, and pity rose—
  "Ah me !" she cried, "I come too late !
Rather than not have sooth'd his woes,
  I would, but may not, share his fate."

She rais'd his hand.   "What hand like this
  Could reach the heart athwart the lyre !
What lips like these return my kiss,
  Or breathe, incessant, soft desire !"

From eve to morn, from morn to eve,
  She gazed his features o'er and o'er,
And those who love and who believe
  May hear her sigh along the shore.

LX.

Is it no dream that I am he
   Whom one awake all night
Rose ere the earliest birds to see,
   And met by dawn's red light ;

Who, when the wintry lamps were spent
   And all was drear and dark,
Against the rugged pear-tree leant
   While ice crackt off the bark ;

Who little heeded sleet and blast,
   But much the falling snow ;
Those in few hours would sure be past,
   His traces *that* might show ;

Between whose knees, unseen, unheard,
   The honest mastiff came,
Nor fear'd he ; no, nor was he fear'd :
   Tell me, am I the same?

O come ! the same dull stars we'll see,
The same o'er-clouded moon.
O come ! and tell me am I he?
O tell me, tell me soon.

LXI.

HERE, where precipitate Spring, with one light
    bound
Into hot Summer's lusty arms, expires,
And where go forth at morn, at eve, at night,
Soft airs that want the lute to play with 'em,
And softer sighs that know not what they want,
Aside a wall, beneath an orange-tree,
Whose tallest flowers could tell the lowlier ones
Of sights in Fiesolè right up above,
While I was gazing a few paces off
At what they seem'd to show me with their nods,
Their frequent whispers and their pointing shoots,
A gentle maid came down the garden-steps
And gathered the pure treasure in her lap.
I heard the branches rustle, and stept forth
To drive the ox away, or mule, or goat,
Such I believed it must be.   How could I
Let beast o'erpower them?   When hath wind or rain
Borne hard upon weak plant that wanted me,

And I (however they might bluster round)
Walkt off? 'Twere most ungrateful: for sweet
    scents
Are the swift vehicles of still sweeter thoughts,
And nurse and pillow the dull memory
That would let drop without them her best stores.
They bring me tales of youth and tones of love,
And 'tis and ever was my wish and way
To let all flowers live freely, and all die
(Whene'er their Genius bids their souls depart)
Among their kindred in their native place.
I never pluck the rose; the violet's head
Hath shaken with my breath upon its bank
And not reproacht me; the ever-sacred cup
Of the pure lily hath between my hands
Felt safe, unsoil'd, nor lost one grain of gold.
I saw the light that made the glossy leaves
More glossy; the fair arm, the fairer cheek
Warmed by the eye intent on its pursuit;
I saw the foot that, altho' half-erect
From its grey slipper, could not lift her up
To what she wanted: I held down a branch
And gather'd her some blossoms; since their hour
Was come, and bees had wounded them, and flies
Of harder wing were working their way thro'
And scattering them in fragments under-foot.

So crisp were some, they rattled unevolved,
Others, ere broken off, fell into shells,
For such appear the petals when detacht,
Unbending, brittle, lucid, white like snow,
And like snow not seen thro', by eye or sun :
Yet every one her gown received from me
Was fairer than the first.   I thought not so,
But so she praised them to reward my care.
I said, "You find the largest."

                             "This indeed,"
Cried she, "is large and sweet."   She held one
    forth,
Whether for me to look at or to take
She knew not, nor did I ; but taking it
Would best have solved (and this she felt) her doubt.
I dared not touch it ; for it seemed a part
Of her own self; fresh, full, the most mature
Of blossoms, yet a blossom ; with a touch
To fall, and yet unfallen.   She drew back
The boon she tender'd, and then, finding not
The ribbon at her waist to fix it in,
Dropt it, as loth to drop it, on the rest.

LXII.

Yes, in this chancel once we sat alone,
O Dorothea! thou wert bright with youth,
Freshness like Morning's dwelt upon thy cheek,
While here and there above the level pews,
Above the housings of the village dames,
The musky fan its groves and zephyrs waved.
I know not why (since we had each our book
And lookt upon it stedfastly) first one
Outran the learned labourer from the desk,
Then tript the other and limpt far behind,
And smiles gave blushes birth, and blushes smiles.
Ah me! where are they flown, my lovely friend!
Two seasons like that season thou hast lain
Cold as the dark-blue stone beneath my feet,
While my heart beats as then, but not with joy.
O my lost friends! why were ye once so dear?
And why were ye not fewer, O ye few?
Must winter, spring, and summer, thus return,
Commemorating some one torn away,
Till half the months at last shall take, with me,
Their names from those upon your scatter'd graves!

LXIII.

IF you please we'll hear another
Timid maid, without the mother.
Unless you are tired, for these
We must travel into Greece.
I know every bay and creek;
Fear no pirate in the Greek.
Here we are, and there is she;
Stand and hide behind the tree.
She will (for I'm grave and grey)
Tell me all she has to say.

   Guest. Violet-eyed little maid!
Of what are you afraid?
   Maid. O! it is Dian's spear,
Sharp-pointed, I most fear.
   Guest. So then you would prefer
Venus, I think, to her?
   Maid. Yes; Venus is so good!
I only wish she would

Keep her sad boy away
Who mocks at all I say.

    Guest. What could he then have heard?

    Maid. Don't ask me—Every word!

    Guest. She has heard *me* ere now.
If you repeat the vow,
I will repeat it too,
And that perhaps may do:
Where there is only one
But little can be done.

    Maid. Perhaps tho' you may blame—
Ah me! I am all flame.

    Guest. With love?

    Maid.   No, no; with shame.

    Guest. Each word that you repeat
Will much abate the heat.

    Maid. Well then—I pray—Don't ask—
I cannot bear the task.

    Guest. Of all the queens above
Fear most the queen of love.
For those alone she cares
Who well repeat their prayers.

    Maid. O then I must, I find,
(But do not look) be blind.
Well, well, now! you shall hear;
But don't come quite so near.

PRAYER.

" Venus ! I fear thy dove
    Is somewhere in my breast :
Yes, yes, I feel him move,
    He will not let me rest.
If he-should ever go,
    I fancy I should sink ;
He fans and wafts me so,
    I think—what do I think ?
O Venus ! thou canst tell—
    'Tis wicked to rebel ! "

'Twas Love : I heard him speak,
But dared not turn my neck ;
I felt his torch so near
And trembled so with fear
I thought I should have died.

   Guest. And was there none beside ?
   Maid. The goddess in white stone
And one young man alone,
His eyes upon the ground,
And lost in thought profound.
Methinks I see him yet,
And never can forget :

For I was almost glad
To see him look so sad,
And gravely disapprove
The mockery of Love.

    Guest. Should Love then reappear,
May that young man be near,
And pray the queen of beauty
To make him do his duty.

LXIV.

THERE is, alas ! a chill, a gloom,
About my solitary room
That will not let one flowret bloom
    Even for you :
The withering leaves appear to say,
" Shine on, shine on, O lovely May !
But we meanwhile must drop away."
    Light ! life ! adieu.

LXV.

MANY may yet recall the hours
That saw thy lover's chosen flowers
Nodding and dancing in the shade
Thy dark and wavy tresses made :
On many a brain is pictured yet
Thy languid eye's dim violet :
But who among them all foresaw
How the sad snows which never thaw
Upon that head one day should lie,
And love but glimmer from that eye.

LXVI.

TO A SPANIEL.

No, Daisy ! lift not up thy ear,
It is not she whose steps draw near.
Tuck under thee that leg, for she
Continues yet beyond the sea,
And thou may'st whimper in thy sleep
These many days, and start and weep.

LXVII.

NEW STYLE.

I VERY much indeed approve
Of maidens moderating love
   Until they've twenty pounds ;
Then Prudence, with a poet's praise,
May loose the laces of their stays,
   And let them quest like hounds.

Peggy, my theme, twelve years ago
(Or better) did precisely so :
   She lived at farmer Spence's ;
She scour'd the pantry, milk'd the cows,
And answer'd every would-be spouse,
   " D'ye think I've lost my senses ? "

Until the twenty pounds were safe,
She tiff'd at Tim, she ran from Ralph,
   Squire nodded—deuce a curtsey !
Sam thought her mopish, Silas proud,
And Jedediah cried aloud,
   " Pray who the devil hurts ye ? "

But now the twenty pounds were got,
She knew the fire to boil the pot,
   She knew the man to trust to.
I'm glad I gave this tidy lass
(Under my roof) a cheerful glass
   (Of water) and a crust too.

Although the seventeenth of May,
It was a raw and misty day
   When Ebenezer Smart,
(The miller's lad of Boxholm-mill)
Having obtained her right good-will
   And prudent virgin heart,

Led her to church: and Joseph Stead
(The curate of said Boxholm) read
   The service; and Will Sands
(The clerk) repeated the response
(They after him) which utter'd once
   Holds fast two plighted hands.

And now they live aside the weir,
And (on my conscience) I declare
   As merrily as larks.
This I can vouch for: 1 went in
One day and sat upon the bin
   While Peggy hemm'd two sarks.

I do not say two sarks entire,
Collar and wristband ; these require
   (I reckon) some time more ;
But mainly two stout sarks, the tail
And fore-flap, stiff as coat of mail
   On knight in days of yore.

I told my sister and our maid
(Anne Waddlewell) how long I stayed
   With Peggy : 'twas until her
Dinner-time : we expect, before
Eight or (at most) nine months are o'er,
   Another little miller.

LXVIII.

PLEASANT it is to wink and sniff the fumes
The little dainty poet blows for us,
Kneeling in his soft cushion at the hearth,
And patted on the head by passing maids.
Who would discourage him? who bid him off?
Invidious or morose!   Enough, to say
(Perhaps too much unless 'tis mildly said)
That slender twigs send forth the fiercest flame,
Not without noise, but ashes soon succeed,
While the broad chump leans back against the stones,
Strong with internal fire, sedately breathed,
And heats the chamber round from morn till night.

LXIX.

TO A PAINTER.

CONCEAL not Time's misdeeds, but on my brow
    Retrace his mark :
Let the retiring hair be silvery now
    That once was dark :
Eyes that reflected images too bright
    Let clouds o'ercast,
And from the tablet be abolisht quite
    The cheerful past.
Yet Care's deep lines should one from waken'd
    Mirth
    Steal softly o'er,
Perhaps on me the fairest of the Earth,
    May glance once more.

The Hellenics.

THE HELLENICS.

DAMÆTAS AND IDA.

DAMÆTAS is a boy as rude
As ever broke maid's solitude.
He watcht the little Ida going
Where the wood-raspberries were growing,
And, under a pretence of fear
Lest they might scratch her arms, drew near,
And, plucking up a stiff grey bent,
The fruit (scarce touching it) he sent
Into both hands : the form they took
Of a boat's keel upon a brook ;
So not a raspberry fell down
To splash her foot or stain her gown.
When it was over, for his pains
She let his lips do off the stains
That were upon two fingers ; he

At first kist two, and then kist three,
And, to be certain every stain
Had vanisht, kist them o'er again.
At last the boy, quite shameless, said
" See ! I have taken out the red !
Now where there's redder richer fruit
Pray, my sweet Ida, let me do 't."
" Audacious creature ! " she cried out,
" What in the world are you about ? "
He had not taken off the red
All over ; on both cheeks 'twas spread ;
And the two lips that should be white
With fear, if not with fear, with spite
At such ill usage, never show'd
More comely, or more deeply glow'd.
Damætas fancied he could move
The girl to listen to his love :
Not he indeed.

Damætas.

For pity's sake !

Ida.

Go ; never more come nigh this brake.

Damætas.

Must I, why must I, press in vain ?

Ida.

Because I hate you.

Damætas.

              Think again,
Think better of it, cruel maid !

Ida.

Well then—because I am afraid.

Damætas.

Look round us : nobody is near.

Ida.

All the more reason for my fear.

Damætas.

Hatred is overcome by you,
And Fear can be no match for two.

ALCIPHRON AND LEUCIPPE.

AN ancient chestnut's blossoms threw
Their heavy odour over two :
Leucippe, it is said, was one,
The other then was Alciphron.
   "Come, come ! why should we stand
     beneath
This hollow tree's unwholesome breath,"
Said Alciphron, "here's not a blade
Of grass or moss, and scanty shade.
Come ; it is just the hour to rove
In the lone dingle shepherds love,
There, straight and tall, the hazel twig
Divides the crooked rock-held fig,
O'er the blue pebbles where the rill
In winter runs, and may run still.
Come then, while fresh and calm the air,
And while the shepherds are not there."

Leucippe.

But I would rather go when they
Sit round about and sing and play.
Then why so hurry me ? for you
Like play and song and shepherds too.

Alciphron.

I like the shepherds very well,
And song and play, as you can tell.
But there is play I sadly fear,
And song I would not have you hear.

Leucippe.

What can it be? what can it be?

Alciphron.

To you may none of them repeat
 The play that you have played with me,
The song that made your bosom beat.

Leucippe.

Don't keep your arm about my waist.

Alciphron.

Might not you stumble?

Leucippe.

                   Well then, do.
But why are we in all this haste?

Alciphron.

To sing.

Leucippe.

          Alas! and not play too?

EUROPA AND HER MOTHER.

Mother.

DAUGHTER ! why roamest thou again so late
Along the damp and solitary shore?

Europa.

I know not.   I am tired of distaf, woof,
Everything.
                              Mother.

                    Yet thou culledst flowers all morn,
And idledst in the woods, mocking shrill birds,
Or clapping hands at limping hares, who stampt
Angrily, and scour'd off.

Europa.

                              I am grown tired
Of hares and birds.   O mother ! had you seen
That lovely creature !   It was not a cow,
And, if it was an ox,* it was unlike

---

* Bulls are never at large in those countries; Europa could
not have seen one.

My father's oxen with the hair rubb'd off
Their necks.

Mother.

A cow it was.

Europa.

Cow it might be—
And yet—and yet—I saw no calf, no font
Of milk: I wish I had; how pleasant 'twere
To draw it and to drink !

Mother.

Europa ! child !
Have we no maiden for such offices ?
No whistling boy?   King's daughters may cull
    flowers,
To place them on the altar of the Gods
And wear them at their festivals.   Who knows ·
But some one of these very Gods may deign
To woo thee? maidens they have wooed less fair.

Europa.

The Gods are very gracious : some of them
Not very constant.

Mother.

Hush !

Europa.

                        Nay, Zeus himself
Hath wandered, and deluded more than one.

Mother.

Fables ! profanest fables !

Europa.

                              Let us hope so.
But I should be afraid of him, and run
As lapwings do when we approach the nest.

Mother.

None can escape the Gods when they pursue.

Europa.

They know my mind, and will not follow me.

Mother.

Consider : some are stars whom they have loved,
Others, the very least of them, are flowers.

Europa.

I would not be a star in winter nights,
In summer days I would not be a flower ;
Flowers seldom live thro' half their time, torn off,
Twirl'd round, and indolently cast aside.

Now, mother, can you tell me what became
Of those who were no flowers, but bent their heads
As pliantly as flowers do?

Mother.
                              They are gone
To Hades.

Europa.
              And left there by Gods they loved
And were beloved by!   Be not such my doom !
Cruel are men, but crueler are Gods.

Mother.

Peace! peace!   Some royal, some heroic, youth
May ask thy father for thy dower and thee.

Europa.

I know not any such, if such there live ;
Royal there may be, but heroic—where?
O mother ! look ! look ! look !

Mother.
                              Thou turnest pale ;
What ails thee ?

Europa.
                    Who in all the house hath dared
To winde those garlands round that grand white
   brow?

So mild, so loving ! Mother ! let me run
And tear them off him : let me gather more
And sweeter.
                    Mother.
            Truly 'tis a noble beast.
See! he comes forward ! see, he rips them off,
Himself !
                    Europa.
            He should not wear them if he would.
Stay there, thou noble creature !   Woe is me !
There are but sandrose, tyme, and snapdragon
Along the shore as far as I can see.
O mother ! help me on his back ; he licks
My foot.   Ah ! what sweet breath !   Now on his side
He lies on purpose for it.   Help me up.

                    Mother.

Well, child !   Indeed he is gentle.   Gods above !
He takes the water !   Hold him tight, Europa !
'Tis well that thou canst swim.
                            Leap off, mad girl !
She laughs !   He lows so loud she hears not me—
But she looks sadder, or my sight is dim—
Against his nostril fondly hangs her hand
While his eye glistens over it, fondly too.
It will be night, dark night, ere she returns.
And that new scarf ! the spray will ruin it !

THE DEATH OF ARTEMIDORA.

" ARTEMIDORA ! Gods invisible,
While thou art lying faint along the couch,
Have tied the sandal to thy slender feet
And stand beside thee, ready to convey
Thy weary steps where other rivers flow.
Refreshing shades will waft thy weariness
Away, and voices like thy own come near
And nearer, and solicit an embrace."
    Artemidora sigh'd, and would have prest
The hand now pressing hers, but was too weak.
Iris stood over her dark hair unseen
While thus Elpenor spake.   He lookt into
Eyes that had given light and life erewhile
To those above them, but now dim with tears
And wakefulness.   Again he spake of joy
Eternal.   At that word, that sad word, *joy*,
Faithful and fond her bosom heav'd once more :
Her head fell back : and now a loud deep sob
Swell'd thro' the darken'd chamber; 'twas not hers.

Note.—A version differing from the above will be found in
Landor's " Pericles and Aspasia," No. lxxxv.

LEONTION, ON TERNISSA'S DEATH
(EPICUROS ALSO DEPARTED).

BEHOLD, behold me, whether thou
Art dwelling with the Shades below
 Or with the Gods above:
With thee were even the Gods more blest—
I wish I could but share thy rest
 As once I shared thy love.

'Twas in this garden where I lean
Against thy tombstone, once the scene
 Of more than mortal bliss,
That loiter'd our Ternissa; sure
She left me that her love was pure;
 It gave not kiss for kiss.

Faint was the blush that overspread
Thro' loosen'd hair her dying head;
 One name she utter'd, one
She sigh'd and wept at; so wilt thou,
If any sorrows reach thee now—
 'Twas not *Leontion.*

Wert thou on earth thou wouldst not chide
The gush of tears I could not hide
　　Who ne'er hid aught from thee.
Willing thou wentest on the way
She went—and am I doom'd to stay?
　　No ; we soon meet, all three.

The flowers she cherisht I will tend,
Nor gather, but above them bend
　　And think they breathe her breath.
Ah, happy flowers ! ye little know
Your youthful nurse lies close below,
　　Close as in life in death.

CLEONE TO ASPASIA.

WE mind not how the sun in the mid-sky
Is hastening on ; but when the golden orb
Strikes the extreme of earth, and when the gulphs
Of air and ocean open to receive him,
Dampness and gloom invade us ; then we think
Ah ! thus is it with Youth.   Too fast his feet
Run on for sight ; hour follows hour ; fair maid
Succeeds fair maid ; bright eyes bestar his couch ;
The cheerful horn awakens him ; the feast,
The revel, the entangling dance, allure,
And voices mellower than the Muse's own
Heave up his buoyant bosom on their wave.
A little while, and then—Ah Youth ! Youth !
    Youth !
Listen not to my words—but stay with me !
When thou art gone, Life may go too ; the sigh
That rises is for thee, and not for Life.

The Last Fruit off an Old Tree.

1853.

I STROVE with none, for none was worth my strife.
Nature I loved, and, next to Nature, Art;
I warmed both hands before the fire of Life;
It sinks, and I am ready to depart.

THE LAST FRUIT OFF AN OLD TREE.

1853.

——•◦•——

I.

ON CATULLUS.

TELL me not what too well I know
About the bard of Sirmio—
    Yes, in Thalia's son
Such stains there are—as when a Grace
Sprinkles another's laughing face
    With nectar, and runs on.

II.

THERE falls with every wedding chime
A feather from the wing of Time.
You pick it up, and say " How fair
To look upon its colours are ! "
Another drops day after day
Unheeded ; not one word you say.
When bright and dusky are blown past,
Upon the hearse there nods the last.

III.

WINTER has changed his mind and fixt to come.
Now two or three snow-feathers at a time
Drop heavily, in doubt if they should drop
Or wait for others to support their fall.

IV.

I ENTREAT you, Alfred Tennyson,
Come and share my haunch of venison.
I have too a bin of claret,
Good, but better when you share it.
Tho' 'tis only a small bin,
There's a stock of it within.
And as sure as I'm a rhymer,
Half a butt of Rudesheimer.
Come ; among the sons of men is one
Welcomer than Alfred Tennyson ?

v.

E. ARUNDELL.

NATURE! thou mayest fume and fret,
There's but one white violet;
Scatter o'er the vernal ground
Faint resemblances around,
Nature ! I will tell thee yet
There's but one white violet.

VI.

GRACEFUL Acacia! slender, brittle,
    I think I know the like of thee;
But thou art tall and she is little—
    What God shall call her his own tree?
Some God must be the last to change her;
    From him alone she will not flee;
O may he fix to earth the ranger,
    And may he lend her shade to me!

VII.

To his young Rose an old man said,
" You will be sweet when I am dead :
Where skies are brightest we shall meet,
And there will you be yet more sweet,
Leaving your winged company
To waste an idle thought on me."

VIII.

THE crysolites and rubies Bacchus brings
 To crown the feast where swells the broad-vein'd brow,
Where maidens blush at what the minstrel sings,
 They who have coveted may covet now.

Bring me, in cool alcove, the grape uncrusht,
 The peach of pulpy cheek and down mature,
Where every voice (but bird's or child's) is husht,
 And every thought, like the brook nigh, runs pure.

IX.

DIALOGUE.

M.

WHY ! who now in the world is this ?
It cannot be the same—I miss
The gift he always brought—a kiss.
Yet still I know my eyes are bright
And not a single hair turn'd white.

L.

O idol of my youth ! upon
That joyous head grey hair there s none,
Nor may there ever be ! grey hair
Is the unthrifty growth of Care,
Which she has planted—you see where.

x.

YEARS, many parti-colour'd years,
   Some have crept on, and some have flown
Since first before me fell those tears
   I never could see fall alone.
Years, not so many, are to come,
   Years not so varied, when from you
One more will fall : when, carried home,
   I see it not, nor hear *adieu.*

XI.

" INSTEAD of idling half my hours,
   I might have learnt the names of flowers
      In gardens, groves, and fields."
   Where then had been the sweet surprise
   That sparkles from those dark-blue eyes?
      Less pleasure knowledge yields.

XII.

NAY, thank me not again for those
Camelias, that untimely rose ;
But if, whence you might please the more
And win the few unwon before,
I sought the flowers you loved to wear,
O'erjoy'd to see them in your hair,
Upon my grave, I pray you, set
One primrose or one violet.
——Stay——-I can wait a little yet.

XIIL

In summer when the sun's mad horses pass
  Thro' more than half the heavens, we sink to rest
In Italy, nor tread the crackling grass,
  But wait until they plunge into the west:
And could not you, Mazzini ! wait awhile?
  The grass is wither'd, but shall spring again;
The Gods, who frown on Italy, will smile
  As in old times, and men once more be men.

XIV.

DEATH stands above me, whispering low
I know not what into my ear:
Of his strange language all I know
Is, there is not a word of fear.

XV.

WEARERS of rings and chains!
Pray do not take the pains
    To set me right.
In vain my faults ye quote ;
I write as others wrote
    On Sunium's hight.

XVI.

ONE lovely name adorns my song,
And, dwelling in the heart,
For ever falters at the tongue,
And trembles to depart.

XVII.

THE fault is not mine if I love you too much,
 I loved you too little too long,
Such ever your graces, your tenderness such,
 And the music the heart gave the tongue.

A time is now coming when Love must be gone,
 Tho' he never abandon'd me yet.
Acknowledge our friendship, our passion disown.
 Our follies (ah can you ?) forget.

XVIII.

LEAF after leaf drops off, flower after flower,
Some in the chill, some in the warmer hour :
Alike they flourish and alike they fall,
And Earth who nourisht them receives them all.
Should we, her wiser sons, be less content
To sink into her lap when life is spent ?

XIX.

TO A CHILD.

POUT not, my little Rose, but take
  With dimpled fingers, cool and soft,
This posy, when thou art awake—
  Mama has worn my posies oft :

This is the first I offer thee,
  Sweet baby ! many more shall rise
From trembling hand, from bended knee,
  Mid hopes and fears, mid doubts and sighs.

Before that hour my eyes will close;
  But grant me, Heaven, this one desire—
In mercy ! may my little Rose
  Never be grafted on a briar.

XX.

LET Youth, who never rests, run by;
    But should each Grace desert the Muse?
Should all that once hath charmed us, fly
    At heavy Age's creaking shoes?
The titter of light Days I hear
    To see so strange a figure come;
Laugh on, light Days, and never fear;
    He passes you; he seeks the tomb.

XXI.

THE wisest of the wise
Listen to pretty lies
   And love to hear 'em told.
Doubt not that Solomon
Listen'd to many a one,
Some in his youth and more when he grew old.

I never was among
The choir of Wisdom's song,
   But pretty lies loved I
As much as any king,
When youth was on the wing,
And (must it then be told?) when youth had quite
   gone by.

Alas ! and I have not
The pleasant hour forgot
   When one pert lady said
" O Walter ! I am quite
Bewilder'd with affright !
I see (sit quiet now) a white hair on your head."

Another more benign
Snipt it away from mine,
  And in her own dark hair
Pretended it was found——
  She lept, and twirl'd it round—
Fair as she was, she never was *so* fair.

XXII.

SEPARATION.

THERE is a mountain and a wood between us,
Where the lone shepherd and late bird have seen us
Morning and noon and even-tide repass.
Between us now the mountain and the wood
Seem standing darker than last year they stood,
And say we must not cross, alas! alas!

XXIII.

IF you no longer love me,
    To friendship why pretend?
Unworthy was the lover,
    Unworthy be the friend.
I know there is another
    Of late prefer'd to me:
Recover'd is my freedom,
    And you again are free.
I've seen the bird that summer
    Deluded from her spray
Return again in winter
    And grieve she flew away.

XXIV.

YOUR last request no fond false hope deceives;
   Your's shall be, Rose! when all your days are o'er,
" The sighs of Zephyrs 'mid the nestling leaves;"
                    " And many more!
Many shall mourn around you, lovely Rose!
   But there must one be absent; there is one
Who griev'd with you in all your little woes—
                He will be gone."

xxv.

ALL is not over while the shade
　　Of parting life, if now aslant,
Rests on the scene whereon it play'd
　　And taught a docile heart to pant.
Autumn is passing by ; his day
　　Shines mildly yet on gather'd sheaves,
And, tho' the grape be pluckt away,
　　Its colour glows amid the leaves.

XXVI.

AGE.

DEATH, tho' I see him not, is near
And grudges me my eightieth year.
Now, I would give him all these last
For one that fifty have run past.
Ah! he strikes all things, all alike,
But bargains: those he will not strike.

XXVII.

TO A LADY ARCHER.

Two Goddesses, not always friends,
　　Are friends alike to you :
To you her bow for trial lends
　　The statelier of the two.

" Let Cupid have it," Venus cries,
　　Diana says " No ! no !
Until your Cupid grows more wise
　　He shall not have my bow."

Her boy was sitting at her side,
　　His bow across his knee.
" Use thou thy own, use this," she cried :
　　" I did, in vain ! " cried he.

" Mother ! we may as well be gone ;
　　No shaft of mine can strike
That figure there, so like thy own,
　　That heart there, so unlike.

ı

XXVIII.

TO VERONA.

VERONA ! thy tall gardens stand erect
Beckoning me upward.   Let me rest awhile
Where the birds whistle hidden in the boughs,
Or fly away when idlers take their place,
Mated as well, conceal'd as willingly ;
Idlers whose nest must not swing there, but rise
Beneath a gleamy canopy of gold,
Amid the flight of Cupids, and the smiles
Of Venus ever radiant o'er their couch.
Here would I stay, here wander, slumber here,
Nor pass into that theatre below
Crowded with their faint memories, shades of joy.
But ancient song arouses me : I hear
Cœlius and Aufilena ; I behold
Lesbia, and Lesbia's linnet at her lip
Pecking the fruit that ripens and swells out
For him whose song the Graces loved the most,
Whatever land, east, west, they visited.

Even he must not detain me : one there is
Greater than he, of broader wing, of swoop
Sublimer.   Open now that humid arch
Where Juliet sleeps the quiet sleep of death,
And Romeo sinks aside her.
                                    Fare ye well,
Lovers !   Ye have not loved in vain : the hearts
Of millions throb around ye.   This lone tomb
One greater than yon walls have ever seen,
Greater than Manto's prophet eye foresaw
In her own child or Rome's, hath hallowed ;
And the last sod or stone a pilgrim knee
Shall press (Love swears it, and swears true) is here.

XXIX.

TO THE NIGHTINGALE.

GALE OF THE NIGHT our fathers call'd thee, bird !
  Surely not rude were they who call'd thee so,
Whether mid spring-tide mirth thy song they heard
  Or whether its soft gurgle melted woe.

They knew not, heeded not, that every clime
  Hath been attemper'd by thy minstrelsy;
They knew not, heeded not, from earliest time
  How every poet's nest was warm'd by thee.

In Paradise's unpolluted bowers
  Did Milton listen to thy freshest strain ;
In his own night didst thou assuage the hours
  When Crime and Tyranny were crown'd again.

Melodious Shelley caught thy softest song,
  And they who heard his music heard not thine;
Gentle and joyous, delicate and strong,
  From the far tomb his voice shall silence mine.

XXX.

AN OLD MAN TO A YOUNG GIRL.

I SAW the arrow quit the bow
To lay thy soaring spirits low,
 And warn'd thee long ere now;
For this thou shunnest me, for this
No more the leap to catch the kiss
 Upon thy calm clear brow.

I pitied thee, well knowing why
The broken song, the book thrown by,
 And Fido's foot put down,
Who looks so sorrowing all the while,
To hear no name, to hope no smile,
 To fear almost a frown.

Lovers who see thy drooping head
In lover's phrase have often said,
 " The lily drives the rose

In shame away from that sweet face,
Yet shall she soon regain her place
   And fresher bloom disclose."

Show them, show one above the rest,
A lily's petals idly prest
   Are firm as they are pure;
Those which but once have given way
Stand up erect no second day,
   No gentlest touch endure.

XXXI.

TO FRANCIS HARE,

**BURIED AT PALERMO, ON THE INSURRECTION OF SICILY
AND NAPLES.**

HARE! thou art sleeping where the sun strikes hot
   On the gold letters that inscribe thy tomb,
And what there passeth round thee knowest not,
   Nor pierce those eyes (so joyous once) the gloom ;

Else would the brightest vision of thy youth
   Rise up before thee, not by Fancy led,
But moving stately at the side of Truth,
   Nor higher than the living stand the dead.

XXXII.

TO YOUTH.

WHERE art thou gone, light-ankled Youth?
   With wing at either shoulder,
And smile that never left thy mouth
   Until the Hours grew colder :

Then somewhat seem'd to whisper near
   That thou and I must part ;
I doubted it ; I felt no fear,
   No weight upon the heart :

If aught befell it, Love was by
   And roll'd it off again ;
So, if there ever was a sigh,
   'Twas not a sigh of pain.

I may not call thee back ; but thou
  Returnest when the hand
Of gentle Sleep waves o'er my brow
  His poppy-crested wand ;

Then smiling eyes bend over mine,
  Then lips once prest invite ;
But sleep hath given a silent sign,
  And both, alas ! take flight.

XXXIII.

TO AGE.

WELCOME, old friend !   These many years
   Have we lived door by door :
The Fates have laid aside their shears
   Perhaps for some few more.

I was indocil at an age
   When better boys were taught,
But thou at length hast made me sage,
   If I am sage in aught.

Little I know from other men,
   Too little they from me,
But thou hast pointed well the pen
   That writes these lines to thee.

Thanks for expelling Fear and Hope,
    One vile, the other vain ;
One's scourge, the other's telescope,
    I shall not see again :

Rather what lies before my feet
    My notice shall engage—
He who hath braved Youth's dizzy heat
    Dreads not the frost of Age.

∨

XXXIV.

ON MUSIC.

MANY love music but for music's sake,
Many because her touches can awake
Thoughts that repose within the breast half-dead,
And rise to follow where she loves to lead.
What various feelings come from days gone by!
What tears from far-off sources dim the eye!
Few, when light fingers with sweet voices play
And melodies swell, pause, and melt away,
Mind how at every touch, at every tone,
A spark of life hath glisten'd and hath gone.

XXXV.

THERE was a lovely tree, I knew
And well remember where it grew,
And very often felt inclined
To hear its whispers in the wind.
One evening of a summer day
I went, without a thought, that way,
And, sitting down, I seem'd to hear
The tree's soft voice, and some one's near.
Yes, sure enough I saw a maid
With wakeful ear against it laid.
Silent was everything around
While thus the tree in quivering sound :
" They pant to cull our fruit, and take
A leaf, they tell us, for our sake,
On the most faithful breast to wear
And keep it, till both perish, there.
Sad pity such kind hearts should pant
So hard ! We give them all they want.
They come soon after and just taste
The fruit, and throw it on the waste.

Again they come, and then pluck off
What poets call our hair, and scoff;
And long ere winter you may see
These leaves fall fluttering round the tree.
They come once more: then, then you find
The root cut round and undermined :
Chains are clencht round it : that fine head,
On which still finer words were said,
Serves only to assist the blow,
And lend them aid to lay it low."
    Methinks I hear a gentle sigh,
And fain would guess the reason why ;
It may have been for what was said
Of fruit and leaves, of root and head.

XXXVI.

TO MIDSUMMER DAY.

CROWN of the Year, how bright thou shinest !
How little, in thy pride, divinest
Inevitable fall ! albeit
We who stand round about foresee it.
Shine on ; shine bravely.   There are near
Other bright children of the Year,
Almost as high, and much like thee
In features and in festive glee :
Some happy to call forth the mower,
And hear his sharpen'd scythe sweep o'er
Rank after rank : then others wait
Before the grange's open gate,
And watch the nodding wane, or watch
The fretted domes beneath the thatch,
Till young and old at once take wing
And promise to return in spring.
Yet I am sorry, I must own,
Crown of the Year ! when thou art gone,

XXXVII.

So then, I feel not deeply ! if I did,
I should have seized the pen and pierced therewith
The passive world !
     And thus thou reasonest ?
Well hast thou known the lover's, not so well
The poet's heart : while that heart bleeds, the hand
Presses it close. Grief must run on and pass
Into near Memory's more quiet shade
Before it can compose itself in song.
He who is agonised and turns to show
His agony to those who sit around,
Seizes the pen in vain : thought, fancy, power,
Rush back into his bosom ; all the strength
Of genius can not draw them into light
From under mastering Grief ; but Memory,
The Muse's mother, nurses, rears them up,
Informs, and keeps them with her all her days.

Dry Sticks Fagotted.

1858.

DRY STICKS FAGOTTED.

1858.

———•◦•———

I.

DEFIANCE.

CATCH her and hold her if you can—
See, she defies you with her fan,
Shuts, opens, and then holds it spread
In threat'ning guise above your head.
Ah! why did you not start before
She reacht the porch and closed the door?
Simpleton! will you never learn
That girls and time will not return;
Of each you should have made the most,
Once gone, they are for ever lost.
In vain your knuckles knock your brow,
In vain will you remember how
Like a slim brook the gamesome maid
Sparkled, and ran into the shade.

II.

TO A FAIR MAIDEN.

FAIR maiden ! when I look at thee
I wish I could be young and free ;
But both at once, ah ! who could be ?

III.

DESTINY UNCERTAIN.

GRACEFULLY shy is yon Gazelle :
  And are those eyes, so clear, so mild,
  Only to shine upon a wild
And be reflected in a shallow well ?
      Ah ! who can tell?

If she grows tamer, who shall pat
  Her neck ? who wreathe the flowers around ?
  Who give the name ? who fence the ground ?
Pondering these things a grave old Dervish sat,
      And sighed, Ah ! who can tell?

IV.

FEAR.

I FEAR a little girl I know;
  Were I but younger I were bolder;
Diana! I would break thy bow
  In twain across her ivory shoulder.

v.

MORN.

SWEET is the Morn where'er it shines,
Whether amid my Tuscan vines,
Or where Sorrento's shadows play
At *hide-and-seek* along the bay,
Or high Amalfi takes its turn,
Until they rest on low Salern.

And here too once the Morn was sweet,
For here I heard the tread of feet
Upon the pebbles wet with dew;
Sweet was the Morn, it breath'd of you,

VI.

TO A CYCLAMEN.

I COME to visit thee again,
My little flowerless cyclamen ;
To touch the hand, almost to press,
That cheer'd thee in thy loneliness.
What could thy careful guardian find
Of thee in form, of me in mind,
What is there in us rich or rare,
To make us claim a moment's care ?
Unworthy to be so carest,
We are but withering leaves at best.

Note.—A version differing from this appeared in the collection
of 1846.

VII.

THE GRATEFUL HEART.

THE grateful heart for all things blesses ;
   Not only joy, but grief endears :
I love you for your few caresses,
   I love you for my many tears.

VIII.

WHERE ARE SIGHS?

UNLESS my senses are more dull
Sighs are become less plentiful.
Where are they all? these many years
Only my own have reacht my ears.

IX.

HOW TO READ ME.

To turn my volumes o'er nor find
  (Sweet unsuspicious friend!)
Some vestige of an erring mind
  To chide or discommend,

Believe that all were loved like you
  With love from blame exempt,
Believe that all my griefs were true
  And all my joys but dreamt.

X.

THE SAGE OF SEVENTEEN.

LITTLE have you to learn from me,
   O sage of seventeen !
Wiser I will not boast to be,
   I cannot to have been.

Go, rather place your hand in hers
   Who acts a mother's part,
And who to all your charms prefers
   Your pure and grateful heart.

Slowly you'll draw it back again
   When Love demands his day;
Pleasure will hardly conquer Pain
   To carry you away.

XI.

UNDER THE LINDENS.

UNDER the lindens lately sat
A couple, and no more, in chat ;
I wondered what they would be at
   Under the lindens.

I saw four eyes and four lips meet,
I heard the words, *How sweet! how sweet!*
Had then the Faeries given a treat
   Under the lindens?

I pondered long and could not tell
What dainty pleased them both so well :
Bees ! bees ! was it your hydromel
   Under the lindens?

XII.

ROSINA.

ROSINA ran down Prior-park,
Joyous and buoyant as a lark.
The little girl, light-heel'd, light-hearted,
Challenged me ; and away we started.
Soon in a flutter she return'd,
And cheek, and brow, and bosom burn'd.
She fairly own'd my full success
In catching her, she could no less,
And said to her mama, who smiled
Yet lovelier on her lovely child,
" You cannot think how fast he ran
For such a very old old man,
He would not kiss me when he might,
And, catching me, he had a right.
Such modesty I never knew,
He would no more kiss me than you."

XIII.

DEATH OF THE DAY.

My pictures blacken in their frames
  As night comes on,
And youthful maids and wrinkled dames
  Are now all one.

Death of the day ! a sterner Death
  Did worse before ;
The fairest form, the sweetest breath,
  Away he bore.

XIV.

ROSINA.

'TIS pleasant to behold
The little leaves unfold
Day after day, still pouting at the Sun,
    Until at last they dare
    Lay their pure bosoms bare :
Of all these flowers I know the sweetest one.

XV.

THE FIG-TREES OF GHERARDESCA.

Ye brave old fig-trees ! worthy pair !
　Beneath whose shade I often lay
To breathe awhile a cooler air,
　And shield me from the darts of day.

Strangers have visited the spot,
　Led thither by my parting song ;
Alas ! the strangers found you not,
　And curst the poet's lying tongue.

Vanisht each venerable head,
　Nor bough nor leaf could tell them where
To look for you, alive or dead ;
　Unheeded was my distant prayer.*

　　　　* Et ficus maneant duo,
　　　　　Semper religiosius
　　　　Servandæ, umbriferum caput
　　　　　Conquassante senecta.

I might have hoped (if hope had ever
   Been mine) that storm or time alone
Your firm alliance would dissever—
   Hath mortal hand your strength o'erthrown?

Before an axe had bitten thro'
   The bleeding bark, some tender thought,
If not for me, at least for you,
   On younger bosoms might have wrought.

Age after age your honeyed fruit
   From boys unseen thro' foliage fell
On lifted apron; now is mute
   The girlish glee! Old friends, farewell!

HEROIC IDYLLS.

WITH ADDITIONAL POEMS.
1863.

WELL I remember how you smiled
  To see me write your name upon
The soft sea-sand—" *O! what a child!*
  You think you're writing upon stone! "
I have since written what no tide
  Shall ever wash away, what men
Unborn shall read o'er ocean wide
  And find Ianthe's name again.

Printed by WALTER SCOTT, *Felling, Newcastle-on-Tyne.*

Small Crown 8vo.

Printed on Antique Laid Paper. Cloth Elegant,
Gilt Edges, Price 3/6.

SUMMER LEGENDS.

By RUDOLPH BAUMBACH.

TRANSLATED BY MRS. HELEN B. DOLE.

This is a collection of charming fanciful stories
translated from the German. In Germany they have
enjoyed remarkable popularity, a large number of
editions having been sold. Rudolph Baumbach deals
with a wonderland which is all his own, though he
suggests Hans Andersen in his simplicity of treatment,
and Heine in his delicacy, grace, and humour. These
are stories which will appeal vividly to the childish
imagination, while the older reader will discern the
satirical or humorous application that underlies them.

London : WALTER SCOTT, 24 Warwick Lane.

The CANTERBURY POETS.

EDITED BY WILLIAM SHARP.

With Introductory Notices by various Contributors.

IN SHILLING MONTHLY VOLUMES, SQUARE 8VO.
Well Printed on Fine Toned Paper, with Red-Line Border, and
Bound in Cloth. Each Volume contains from 300 to 350 pages.

Cloth, Red Edges	- 1s.	*Red Roan, Gilt Edges*, 2s. 6d.
Cloth, Uncut Edges -	- 1s.	*Pad Morocco, Gilt Edges* - 5s.

VOLUMES ALREADY ISSUED.

Christian Year.
Coleridge.
Longfellow.
Campbell.
Shelley.
Wordsworth.
Blake.
Whittier.
Poe.
Chatterton.
Burns. Poems.
Burns. Songs.
Marlowe.
Keats.
Herbert.
Victor Hugo.
Cowper.
Shakespeare:
Songs, Poems, and Sonnets.
Emerson.
Sonnets of this Century.
Whitman.
Scott. Marmion, etc.
Scott. Lady of the Lake, etc.
Praed.
Hogg.
Goldsmith.
Mackay's Love Letters.
Spenser.
Children of the Poets.
Ben Jonson.

Byron (2 Vols.)
Days of the Year.
Sonnets of Europe.
Allan Ramsay.
Sydney Dobell.
Pope.
Helne.
Beaumont and Fletcher.
Bowles, Lamb, etc.
Early English Poetry.
Sea Music.
Herrick.
Ballades and Rondeaus.
Irish Minstrelsy.
Milton's Paradise Lost.
Jacobite Ballads.
Australian Ballads.
Moore's Poems.
Border Ballads.
Song-Tide.
Odes of Horace.
Ossian.
Elfin Music.
Southey.
Chaucer.
Poems of Wild Life.
Paradise Regained.
Crabbe.
Dora Greenwell.
Goethe's Faust.
American Sonnets.
Landor's Poems.

London: WALTER SCOTT, 24 Warwick Lane, Paternoster Row.

THE CAMELOT SERIES.

CLOTH, CUT OR UNCUT EDGES.

New Comprehensive Edition of Favourite Prose Works.

Edited by ERNEST RHYS.

In SHILLING Monthly Volumes, Crown 8vo.

VOLUMES ALREADY ISSUED.

Romance of King Arthur.
Thoreau's Walden.
Confessions of an English Opium-Eater.
Landor's Conversations.
Plutarch's Lives.
Browne's Religio Medici.
Essays and Letters of P. B. Shelley.
Prose Writings of Swift.
My Study Windows.
Great English Painters.
Lord Byron's Letters.
Essays by Leigh Hunt.
Longfellow's Prose.
Great Musical Composers
Marcus Aurelius.
Specimen Days in America.
White's Natural History.
Captain Singleton.
Essays by Mazzini.

Prose Writings of Heine.
Reynolds' Discourses.
The Lover: Papers of Steele and Addison.
Burns's Letters.
Volsunga Saga.
Sartor Resartus.
Writings of Emerson.
Seneca's Morals.
Democratic Vistas.
Life of Lord Herbert.
English Prose.
The Pillars of Society.
Fairy and Folk Tales.
Epictetus.
Essays on English Poets.
Essays of Dr. Johnson.
Essays of Wm. Hazlitt.
Landor's Pentameron, &c.
Poe's Tales and Essays.
Vicar of Wakefield.
Political Orations.

The Series is issued in two styles of Binding—Red Cloth, Cut Edges; and Dark Blue Cloth, Uncut Edges. Either Style, 1s.

London: WALTER SCOTT, 24 Warwick Lane, Paternoster Row.

Windsor Series of Poetical Anthologies.

*Printed on Antique Paper. Crown 8vo. Bound in Blue Cloth,
each with suitable Emblematic Design on Cover, Price 3/6.
Also in various Calf and Morocco Bindings.*

Women's Voices. An Anthology of the most
Characteristic Poems by English, Scotch, and Irish Women.
Edited by Mrs. William Sharp.

Sonnets of this Century. With an Exhaustive
Essay on the Sonnet. Edited by William Sharp.

The Children of the Poets. An Anthology from
English and American Writers of Three Centuries. Edited
by Professor Eric S. Robertson.

Sacred Song. A Volume of Religious Verse.
Selected and arranged, with Notes, by Samuel Waddington.

A Century of Australian Song. Selected and
Edited by Douglas B. W. Sladen, B.A., Oxon.

Jacobite Songs and Ballads. Selected and
Edited, with Notes, by G. S. Macquoid.

Irish Minstrelsy. Edited, with Notes and Introduction, by H. Halliday Sparling.

The Sonnets of Europe. A Volume of Trans-
lations. Selected by Samuel Waddington.

Early English and Scottish Poetry. Selected
and Edited, with Introduction, by H. Macaulay Fitzgibbon.

Ballads of the North Countrie. Edited, with
Introduction, by Graham R. Tomson.

Songs and Poems of the Sea. An Anthology
of Poems Descriptive of the Sea. Edited by Mrs. William
Sharp.

Songs and Poems of Fairyland. An Anthology
of English Fairy Poetry. Edited by A. E. Waite.

Songs and Poems of the Great Dominion.
Edited by W. D. Lighthall, of Montreal.

London: WALTER SCOTT, 24 Warwick Lane, Paternoster Row.

OUR
AMERICAN
COUSINS.

By W. E. ADAMS.

The author brings to his work acute penetration, a keen observation, a graphic picturesque style of presenting his impressions, and a quiet humour that finds expression in quoting amusing scraps from newspaper stories and sayings that aptly illustrate the case in point.—*New York Herald.*

That Mr. Adams is a person with a power for observing closely, describing impartially, and arriving at conclusions sustained by his process of argument, cannot be doubted by those who read his interesting work.—*New York Evening Telegram.*

We can heartily recommend Mr. Adams's book to those Englishmen who want to know something about America.—*Saturday Review*, 13th October 1883.

. . . We can say emphatically and truthfully of Mr Adams's book that it is by far the best work of its kind we have yet seen.—*Knowledge.*

. . . Altogether, it is a sober, sensible book, by a level-headed observer of men and things.—*Pall Mall Gazette*, 12th November 1883.

People who want to know what Americans are like, and how they live, cannot do better than consult Mr. Adams's work, in which they will not find a single tedious page.—*Scotsman*, 13th September.

London : WALTER SCOTT, 24 Warwick Lane, Paternoster Row.

Crown 8vo, Paper Cover, Price Sixpence.

THE TURKISH BATH:

ITS HISTORY AND USES.

BY

FREDERIC C. COLEY, M.D.

CONTENTS :—The History of the Turkish Bath—How to take a Turkish Bath—Rules for the Turkish Bath—The Theory of the Turkish Bath.

London : WALTER SCOTT, 24 Warwick Lane, Paternoster Row.

RECENT VOLUMES OF VERSE.

ROMANTIC BALLADS AND POEMS OF PHANTASY.

By WILLIAM SHARP. Second Edition. 3s.

Author of "The Human Inheritance," "Earth's Voices," "Dante Gabriel Rossetti: a Record and a Study," "Shelley: A Biographical Study," "Life of Heine," etc.

"Verse of this kind is so exceptional that one can only speak of it in terms of grateful appreciation. We shall naturally look for more of the same quality from the same source; but no fountain, however affluent, yields such streams every day."—*The Academy.*

CAROLS, SONGS, AND BALLADS.

By JOSEPH SKIPSEY.

New Edition. Crown 8vo, blue cloth, 3s. 6d.

"Mr. Skipsey can find music for every mood, whether he is dealing with the real experiences of the pitman, or with the imaginative experiences of the poet, and his verse has a rich vitality about it. In these latter days of shallow rhymes, it is pleasant to come across some one to whom poetry is a passion, not a profession."—*Pall Mall Gazette.*

DEATH'S DISGUISES AND OTHER SONNETS.

By FRANK T. MARZIALS. Parchment limp, 3s.

"Mr. Frank T. Marzials' charming and finely wrought little book of poems."—*Scotsman.*

"IT IS THYSELF."

By MARK ANDRÉ RAFFALOVICH. Crown 8vo, 3s 6d.

Author of "In Fancy Dress," "Cyril and Lionel," etc.

London: WALTER SCOTT, 24 Warwick Lane.

Crown 8vo, Cloth,

PRICE ONE SHILLING.

ELOCUTION

BY

T. R. WALTON PEARSON, M.A.

Of St. Catharine's College, Cambridge,

AND

FREDERIC WILLIAM WAITHMAN,

*Lecturer on Elocution in the Leeds and
Bradford Institutes.*

London: WALTER SCOTT, 24 Warwick Lane, Paternoster Row.

Crown 8vo.   Paper Cover, 1s.   *Cloth*, 2s.

WOMEN AND MEN OF THE DAY,
A COLLECTION OF SOCIAL SKETCHES
By LILLIE HARRIS.

OUR YOUNG LADIES.   OUR YOUNG MEN.
OUR MARRIED LADIES. OUR MARRIED MEN.

"There is much sound sense in the suggestions offered to young persons of the gentler sex, who would do well to take to heart the somewhat sharp, though not unkindly, criticism."
—*Lancet.*

"'Our young men' get it hot and heavy from Miss Harris—if she is a Miss Harris, or if the writer of these pungent little articles be a lady at all.   We are not inclined to doubt it because the articles *are* pungent and clever, but because Miss Harris betrays an intimate acquaintance with all masculine ways that puzzles us.   However, whether the author be a man or woman, she—we shall use the feminine pronoun on trust—is gifted with a ready and satirical pen, which is yet never anything but good-natured.   Our young men will almost overlook her hard-hitting for the sake of the good, honest laugh she gives them, even at their own expense."—*Glasgow Herald.*

"The æsthetic, social, and other 'fashions' of the young lady of the day are dealt with in a very trenchant and effective manner, and though the satire is sometimes severe, it is withal good-natured and genial.   The amusements, manners, flirtations, reading, etc., of the sex come in for a good deal of kindly criticism, and the author seems to have had a deal of experience of the matters on which she writes.   This little work will prove not only interesting but instructive reading to those concerned ; and may possibly prove of interest to our 'young gentlemen' also."—*Service Gazette.*

London : WALTER SCOTT, 24 Warwick Lane, Paternoster Row.

Crown 8vo, Cloth,

PRICE ONE SHILLING.

ELOCUTION

BY

T. R. WALTON PEARSON, M.A.

Of St. Catharine's College, Cambridge,

AND

FREDERIC WILLIAM WAITHMAN,

Lecturer on Elocution in the Leeds and Bradford Institutes.

London: WALTER SCOTT, 24 Warwick Lane, Paternoster Row.

Crown 8vo.   Paper Cover, 1s.   *Cloth*, 2s.

WOMEN AND MEN OF THE DAY,
A COLLECTION OF SOCIAL SKETCHES
By LILLIE HARRIS.

OUR YOUNG LADIES.   OUR YOUNG MEN.
OUR MARRIED LADIES. OUR MARRIED MEN.

"There is much sound sense in the suggestions offered to young persons of the gentler sex, who would do well to take to heart the somewhat sharp, though not unkindly, criticism." —*Lancet.*

"'Our young men' get it hot and heavy from Miss Harris—if she is a Miss Harris, or if the writer of these pungent little articles be a lady at all. We are not inclined to doubt it because the articles *are* pungent and clever, but because Miss Harris betrays an intimate acquaintance with all masculine ways that puzzles us. However, whether the author be a man or woman, she—we shall use the feminine pronoun on trust—is gifted with a ready and satirical pen, which is yet never anything but good-natured. Our young men will almost overlook her hard-hitting for the sake of the good, honest laugh she gives them, even at their own expense."—*Glasgow Herald.*

"The æsthetic, social, and other 'fashions' of the young lady of the day are dealt with in a very trenchant and effective manner, and though the satire is sometimes severe, it is withal good-natured and genial. The amusements, manners, flirtations, reading, etc., of the sex come in for a good deal of kindly criticism, and the author seems to have had a deal of experience of the matters on which she writes. This little work will prove not only interesting but instructive reading to those concerned; and may possibly prove of interest to our 'young gentlemen' also."—*Service Gazette.*

London: WALTER SCOTT, 24 Warwick Lane, Paternoster Row.

www.ingramcontent.com/pod-product-compliance
Lightning Source LLC
Chambersburg PA
CBHW031357270326

41929CB00010BA/1213